Praise for *The Broken Way*

What you need to know about Ann Voskamp: after the stunning success of *One Thousand Gifts*, she has chosen to decline the mantle of spiritual guru and instead to become even more intimately vulnerable. In this book, she helps us slow down, stop time, and allow gritty faith to penetrate, expose, and bring the hint of healing to the mess of daily life. For all imperfect people—in other words, for all of us—she offers a compassionate and wise way forward to help navigate our broken world.

PHILIP YANCEY, editor-at-large, *Christianity Today*

In *The Broken Way*, a deeply personal revelation, Ann Voskamp leads us on a journey toward embracing and celebrating the brokenness in each of us. The passionate words that pour from her soul will make you weep and shout hallelujah at the same time.

KAY WARREN, Saddleback Church,
Lake Forest, California

There are only a handful of authors in the whole world who I try to find and read every last word they've ever written. Ann Voskamp is one of those. *The Broken Way* is no exception, as Ann does what she does best—articulating the incredible grace of Jesus in a profound way that makes all of us go YES! but had no words for before. This must-read book will give life to any weary soul.

JEFFERSON BETHKE, *New York Times* bestselling author of *Jesus > Religion* and *It's Not What You Think*

Ann Voskamp is convincing that there is nothing broken that cannot be restored by making the living Christ present. She provides a stunningly fresh treatment of a subject so often littered with clichés. My favorite phrase is, "Fight back the dark with doxology . . . doxology can detox the day."

EUGENE H. PETERSON, emeritus professor of
spiritual theology, Regent College, Vancouver, BC

I read *The Broken Way* with tears streaming down my face, my spirit crying out, *"YES, YES, YES, YES!"* Few authors have impacted my own life like Ann Voskamp. If we can live out the truth contained within *The Broken Way*, I believe we will reach and impact our generation like never before. So powerful. So prophetic. So profound. Please read this book.

CHRISTINE CAINE, founder of A21 and Propel Women

The Broken Way is the most honest and beautiful healing balm for an aching heart. The authenticity and grace from which Ann Voskamp writes are refreshing and life-giving. This book is a true gift from God!

LYSA TERKEURST, *New York Times* bestselling
author and president of Proverbs 31 Ministries

Ann Voskamp's skill with words, her tenderness with hearts—it is incomparable. Life can leave us looking for an exit, a window. Ann has a hand on the curtain. She has a way of releasing light, just enough to chase shadows and give hope.

MAX LUCADO, pastor and bestselling author

Most of us want to run away from our brokenness. Ann Voskamp runs right into it, sharing the shattered pieces of her own life to help us acknowledge the shards we may be sifting through. Ann helps us see God's good purpose in all of it, and how He guides us, not around the pain, but through it. Beautifully written, *The Broken Way* offers a generous measure of hope, filled with Ann's tender honesty and God's powerful truth.

LIZ CURTIS HIGGS, bestselling author
of *Bad Girls of the Bible*

In the way only she can, Ann Voskamp invites us to discover that the whole life begins in our brokenness. Ann knows what it means to be broken. She knows what it means to have scars. This isn't her theory; it's her heartbeat. Lean in to this book, and listen for it.

LAUREN CHANDLER, singer/songwriter
and author of *Steadfast Love*

Ann Voskamp penetrates the soul with words that arrest us, convict us, and compel us to the arms of our Father. Ann Voskamps come along once in a generation. We best pay attention.

GABE LYONS, author of *Good Faith*

ALSO BY ANN VOSKAMP

THE
BROKEN
WAY

A Daring Path into the Abundant Life

ANN VOSKAMP

 ZONDERVAN®

ZONDERVAN

The Broken Way
Copyright © 2016 by Ann Morton Voskamp

Requests for information should be addressed to:
Zondervan, *3900 Sparks Dr. SE, Grand Rapids, Michigan 49546*

ISBN 978-0-310-31858-3 (hardcover)

ISBN 978-0-310-34927-3 (signature edition)

ISBN 978-0-310-34656-2 (international trade paper edition)

ISBN 978-0-310-31862-0 (audio)

ISBN 978-0-310-31859-0 (epub)

Published in association with William K. Jensen Literary Agency, 119 Bampton Court, Eugene, Oregon 97404.

Cover design: Curt Diepenhorst
Cover photo: Mary Anne Morgan
Interior imagery: PhotoDisc / Siede Preis
Interior design: Kait Lamphere

First Printing August 2016 / Printed in the United States of America

To Mine . . . who never gave up on the broken—
and to every single one who carries
their own unspoken broken—
these pages had to be for you—
the tracing of scars.

Contents

One

What to Do with Your One Broken Heart

The very thing we are afraid of, our brokenness,
is the door to our Father's heart.

PAUL MILLER

The day I cut up the inner softness of my arm with a shard of glass, the whole thick weight of hell's pressing against my chest.

A mourning dove coos from the top of the lilac tree right outside the back door. West of the barn, my dad had yanked the steering wheel of that old International tractor, geared the engine down, and turned at the end of the field.

And I had stood, out on the back porch, all of sixteen, and let go of those glass jars. Dozens of them. I stood with broken glass shattered around my feet. No one could tell me how to get the dark, the fear, the ache, the hell out of me. No one could tell me how to find the place where you always felt safe and secure and held. Kneeling, I'd picked up one of the shards, dragged its sharp edge across my skin, relieved by the red line slowly seeping up, like you could drain yourself out of pain. I'd try to cut my way through the hurt down to the core of things. Who doesn't know what it's like to smile thinly and say you're fine when you're not, when you're almost faint with pain? There isn't one of us not bearing the wounds from our own bloody battles.

There isn't one of us who isn't cut right from the beginning.

All of us get pushed from safe wombs out into this holy mess. All of us need someone to catch us and hold us right from the beginning, and for one sacred moment, every single one of us is cupped. And then they cut that one thick umbilical cord. You can spend a lifetime feeling pushed out, cut off, abandoned—inexplicably alone.

What in God's holy name do you do when it feels like you're broken and cut up, and love has failed, and you've failed, and you feel like Somebody's love has failed you?

Dad had just kept breaking open the earth, just kept planting wheat seeds, thousands of them. They grew.

The wheat across the fields to the west waits in willing surrender.

Later, he'd cut down the harvest. I never once told him how I cut. Never once told him how, in that moment when the jars shatter, when the shimmer of glass slides through your skin, there's this exhaling moment when you feel the relief of not hiding anymore. Not acting, not for one more mocking minute that everything is just bloody fine.

I knelt down and held the shards in my hand and turned the edges over.

Not one thing in your life is more important than figuring out how to live in the face of unspoken pain.

It may have been more than two decades since my cutting throughout my teens, but standing there in the kitchen this older, more battle weary, more broken woman, looking out over wheat fields of our own, I'm overwhelmed by how my skin's starved again for the cutting, for the breaking edge of glass again. How my wrists want to feel that sharp, bleeding relief and hemorrhage out of all this pain.

And that's the razor edge of things right there: Our oldest daughter, she's just laid it all out in stark details, how intimately familiar she is with the very same struggle and strangle of silent anxiety and lies of unworthiness that I've spent my entire life wrestling. I feel a door opening on my very own private nightmare, and I'm kinda gaping just to breathe. *Keep holding on to the edge of the counter, keep trying to stand, keep trying to figure out how to hold on and let go.* Feeling the weight of your failure feels worse than taking a knife to your own pulpy heart. When you somehow pass your brokenness onto your own people, why does it hurt in a way physical pain never could? And for weeks, I've been falling hard in hidden ways, in ways I can't even find words to speak out loud, and seen the depth of my own brokenness in ways I would never have imagined. There's this ember that's burning up my throat. The wheat's bending into the wind, moving with the wind. *I don't know the way out of all this.*

I've changed. Life's changed and I've changed and five years ago I didn't know how to love or to feel love, had to count all the ways, a thousand ways, that God always loves me so I could even begin to learn how to let myself be loved—and somehow along the way, brushing up against hurting people and stories and places, I've changed into this woman who's embraced a love so large it's broken my heart in a thousand aching places. *Don't we all want to change? What do you do when it feels like everything's changed?* It's a strange thing to find out your heart can explode with love and suffering and find out they're kin in ways we don't care to admit. *I don't know the way to put all these broken pieces back into place. Maybe that's the point?*

NOT ONE THING

IN YOUR LIFE

IS MORE IMPORTANT

THAN FIGURING OUT

HOW TO LIVE

IN THE FACE OF

UNSPOKEN PAIN.

Maybe this broken way is making something new. *He is making all things new.*

So how do you silence the demon-lies that won't stop crawling up the sides of your mind and really believe that? How do you bind up the slow bleeding of your one broken heart and still believe wounded warriors win, still believe that there is no remission of sins or the crossing of finish lines without things getting downright bloody, still believe that scars and wounds and broken places might become you and become who you are? And maybe this is how all the brokenhearted misfits finally fit. All I can feel is this unspoken brokenness splintering through me. What do you do if you're struggling to remember who you really are?

I'm not enough for any of this.

Not enough for anything I'm doing, for anything I am facing, for anyone I am facing. *Not enough for my life.*

Standing here in the kitchen, looking out at the wheat fields, I don't know there will be this funeral and coffin coming. That there will be this diagnosis coming that would stick its face in ours and we'd never get to turn away. That even more desperately broken parenting days were coming. But I know a mother's labor and delivery never ends, and you have to keep remembering to breathe.

I couldn't know yet the way to the higher up and deeper in and that vulnerability would beg me to just break open and let trust in. *Let the abundance of God in.*

I just know that—old scars can break open like fresh wounds and your unspoken broken can start to rip you wide open and maybe the essence of all the questions is: how in the holy name of God do you live with your one broken heart?

Cutting the thin whites of my inner arms through my gangly teen years was this silent scream for bloody answers.

Cora-Beth Martin, she'd cut her wrists on the sharp edge of the paper towel dispenser at the school, rubbing her wrists back and forth, wild for a way to get away from that old guy rubbing himself up against her in the locked dark every night.

Ema Winters, she'd stopped eating. Maybe if she didn't open her mouth, the pain wouldn't get in and the ache of everything would waste away off her bones.

I'd sat in some counselor's sticky office on a hot June afternoon, twisting this bent-up high school ring round and round my knuckle, watched her lean forward, her stringy brown hair falling like a veil, and heard her say point-blank that I showed all the symptoms of suffering enmeshment and emotional abuse, the words punching hard up into my diaphragm, and I can only shake my head. *No. No. No.* Every breath hurts along all the gravel roads home. If I don't inhale, that woman's words can't get to me. I park the pickup out by the barn and rummage through the garbage bin, desperate for a jar.

For the smooth skin of my inner arm.

Dad always said that the day my little sister was killed, the Terpstras had their John Deere tractor plowing the field right across from the house, breaking up the earth. Right across from where we'd watched that delivery truck knock her over like some flimsy pylon and crush her, us standing there like impotent shadows, watching her ebb away. Dad said they'd just kept breaking up the earth, when his world had stopped dead. He said he'd wanted to break their necks for not stopping and getting off that tractor, when he could do nothing to save the broken body of his little girl or find a way out of the brokenness cutting up this world. Sometimes you can feel the crush of it on your brittle rib cage. Great grief isn't made to fit inside your body. It's why your heart breaks. If you haven't felt this yet, it may be, God forbid, that someday you will.

There's absolutely no tidy pattern as to who gets pain and who gets peace. How had I not seen that the brokenness of this world is so all-encompassing that it encompasses all of us?

The wheat stands behind the orchard, turning itself into pure gold.

This is the deal we all get: guaranteed suffering. We all get it. It is coming, unstoppable, like time.

There are graves coming, there is dark coming, there is heartbreak coming. We are not in control, and we never were. One moment you're picking up balls of crusty dirty socks strewn across the bedroom floor, and the next moment you're picking up the pieces of your one shattered life.

How do you live with your one broken heart?

All the wheat looks like an onyx sea. The trees at the edge of the field reach up like a lyric scratched across the sky. It's like that line of Hugo's from *Les Misérables*: "There is one spectacle grander than the sea, that is the sky; there is one spectacle grander than the sky, that is the interior of the soul."[1] *How does the interior of your soul live with broken things, through broken things?*

Jesus died crying.

Jesus died of a broken heart. Those words were still warm on His cracked lips: "My God, my God, why have you forsaken me?"[2] The movement of a life of faith is always toward answering that singular question. Read the headlines. Read the obituaries. Read people's eyes. Isn't the essence of the Christian life to answer that one, nail-sharp question: *God, why in this busted-up world have You abandoned me?*

I can see that question hanging over our farm table, up in the gable, from that framed canvas of a thousand little broken squares of color. In the semiabstract painting, there's no tidy pattern, just light and dark bleeding into this subtle suggestion of Jesus hanging on the cross. He's hoarse with the begging, for Himself, for us: "God, why have You abandoned me?" And He surfaces in the patches of color, the broken brushstrokes, the silhouette of Him visible in the chaos—Christ entering all this chaos.

There is the truth: Blessed—lucky—are those who cry. Blessed are those who are sad, who mourn, who feel the loss of what they love—because they will be held by the One who loves them. There is a strange and aching happiness only the hurting know—for they shall be held.

And, by God, we're the hurting beggars begging: Be close to the brokenhearted. Save the crushed in spirit. Somehow make suffering turn this evil against itself, so that a greater life rises from the dark. *God, somehow.*

I was eighteen, with scars across my wrists, when I'd heard a pastor tell a whole congregation that he had once "lived next to a loony bin." I'd looked at the floor when everyone laughed. They didn't know how I had left my only mama behind the locked doors of psychiatric wards more than a few times. When they laughed, I felt the blood drain away from my face, and I'd wanted to stand up and howl, "It is not the healthy who need a doctor, but the sick."[3]

I'd wanted to stand up and beg: *When the church isn't for the suffering and broken, then the church isn't for Christ.* Because Jesus, with His pierced side, is always on the side of the broken. Jesus always moves into places moved with grief. Jesus always seeks out where the suffering is, and that's where Jesus stays. The wound in His side proves that Jesus is always on the side of the suffering, the wounded, the busted, the broken.

I believed this then and believe it now and I'd say I know

it to be true—but there is more than believing—there is living what you believe. *Do I really?*

What I wanted that Sunday when I was eighteen, sitting in a church of laughter mocking the hurting, was for all the broken to say it together, as one body, to say it for the hurting and broken and to say it to each other, because there is not even one of us who hasn't lost something, who doesn't fear something, who doesn't ache with some unspoken pain. I wanted us to say it to each other until it is the bond of a promise we cannot break:

The body of Christ doesn't offer you some clichés, but something to cling to—right here in our own scarred hands.

His body doesn't offer some platitudes, but some place for your pain—right here in our own offered time.

His body doesn't offer some excuses, but we'll be an example—right here in our bending down and washing your wounds.

And we are His and He is ours, so we are each other's, and we will never turn away.

But instead I'd heard preached what Jesus never had: some pseudo-good news that if you just pray well, sing well, worship well, live well, and give lots, well, you get to take home a mind and body that are well. *That's not how the complex beauty of life breaks open.*

The real Jesus turns to our questions of why—why this brokenness, why this darkness?—and says, "You're asking the wrong question. You're looking for someone to blame. There is no such cause-effect here."[4] "This happened so the power of God could be seen in him."[5]

There's brokenness that's not about blame. There's brokenness that makes a canvas for God's light. There's brokenness that makes windows straight into souls. Brokenness happens in a soul so the power of God can happen in a soul.

Isn't this what Mother Teresa laid out on the table: "There is such terrible darkness within me, as if everything was dead . . . I do not know how deeper will this trial go—how much pain and suffering it will bring to me. This does not worry me anymore. I leave this to Him as I leave everything else . . . Let Him do with me whatever He wants as He wants for as long as He wants if my darkness is light to some soul."[6]

The sky is this fading grey across the fields, emptying across the rolling hills. But flames of light still catch in the far edge of the waving wheat, burning up the maples at the fringe of the woods.

The lit trees don't move in the wind, certain they are safe, that we are all safe.

I wash and dry the white porcelain pitcher at the sink. That moment, the edges of me, feel fragile. Not wanting one more thing to crack. Not wanting to crack one thing more.

Is there a grace that can bury the fear that your faith isn't big enough and your faults are too many? A grace that washes your dirty wounds and wounds the devil's lies? A grace that embraces you before you prove anything—and after you've done everything wrong? A grace that holds you when everything is breaking down and falling apart—and whispers that everything is somehow breaking free and falling together.

I had wanted someone to reach over to me at eighteen, sit in that church pew next to me, someone to touch my shoulder, to steady things and say: "Shame is a bully but grace is a shield. You are safe here."

What if the busted and broken hearts could *feel* there's a grace that holds us and calls us Beloved and says we belong and no brokenness ever has the power to break us away from being safe? What if we *experienced* the miracle of grace that can touch all our wounds?

I wanted to write it on walls and on the arms scarred with wounds, make it the refrain we sing in the face of the dark and broken places: No shame. No fear. No hiding. All's grace. It's always safe for the suffering here. You can struggle and you can wrestle and you can hurt and we will be here. Grace will meet you here; grace, perfect comfort, will always be served here.

How to remember there's a Doctor in the house who "binds up the brokenhearted,"[7] a Wounded Healer who uses nails to buy freedom and crosses to resurrect hope and He never treats those who hurt on the inside as less than those who hurt on the outside. How do I remember that: "Hearts are broken in ten thousand ways, for this is a heart-breaking world; and Christ is good at healing all manner of heart-breaks."[8] How do I stand a thousand nights out on the creaking porch, lean over the pine rail, and look up: The same hand that unwraps the firmaments of winging stars wraps liniments around the wounded heart; the One whose breath births galaxies into being births healing into the heart of the broken.

I put the porcelain pitcher on the barn board shelf by the farm table. All of us in a heart-breaking world, we are the fellowship of the broken like that painting over the table. Over all of us is the image of the wounded God, the God who breaks open and bleeds with us.

How do you live with your one broken heart? All I can think is—only the wounds of God can heal our wounds. This is the truth, and I feel the rising of it: suffering is healed by suffering, wounds are healed by wounds. It jars me, shatters my fears into the softness of Him: bad brokenness is healed by His good brokenness. *Bad brokenness is broken by good brokenness.*

What in the world does that even mean? And could I find out simply by daring to discover it—some new dare.

Like a brokenhearted way to . . . abundance?

Shalom had come to me sitting there at the sticky farm table, come with her heart cut out of white paper.

She brought the paper heart and this roll of tape to me and asks, "Will you do it, Mama? I can't make it work." And she holds out a roll of mangled clear tape.

I'm sitting there bent over her brother and his spelling words.

"What are you trying to do, sweet?" Tape it in half? Tape it to the wall?

"I just want the heart taped to me. Just right here." Shalom staccatos her finger off her chest.

Her brother's erasing his paper too hard, wearing a hole right through. Trying to erase everything he'd got wrong.

"Just tape it right here." Shalom points just above her own thrumming heart.

"And why are we doing this exactly?" I'm on my knees in front of her, half smiling, looking up into her face, my thumb smoothing the tape line of this exposed heart.

I asked the question, even though we'd just talked it over that morning at breakfast, about how we need to give love to others. So of course, she's trying to put into practice her mother's half-baked words and I'm going to have to tell her this is bold and brilliant, making herself into a walking sign of my little breakfast lecture.

Usually I'm the one cupping her face in my hands, but now she's got me here, kneeling in front of her, so she takes my face into her hands. And she bends so close I can feel her breath warm.

"We need to tape hearts right to us, Mama. So we always know." She strokes my cheek. "So we always know His love's around us everywhere."

His love's around us everywhere.

If only we could all wear a heart right across the center of us so there was always this knowing: God has not forgotten you. God has not abandoned you. God's love is around you everywhere. When you feel in your marrow how you're His Beloved, you do more than look for signs of His love in the world, more than have a sign of His love; you actually become a sign of His love.

Her palms warm on my cheeks, I feel it in one long moment—how we can be held again. I want her to never stop holding me. Maybe this is what real love feels like—a slight breaking of the heart, and a slight breathless surprise at finding yourself put back together into a kind of wholeness. *Shalom.*

Shalom looks down, smooths out her paper heart, white and larger than life (because isn't love always larger than life, and isn't that always the point?). And then the inevitable happens, what always happens: the heart breaks, rips right down the center, just where she tried to smooth everything out. I'd swallowed hard.

How in the world do you live with your one broken heart?

Shalom looks down at hers. I am waiting for her to brim and overrun.

"It's all okay." She finds the right first words. She holds the torn bit of her paper heart out to me. "Maybe the love gets in easier right where the heart's broke open?"

I blink at her, replaying the moment.

Maybe the love gets in easier right where the heart's broke open.

I pull her in close, gently kiss her in the middle of her perfect little forehead—and off she goes with her one broken heart. And I'd sat there in the wake of her, waking: maybe you can live a full and beautiful life in spite of the great and terrible moments that will happen right inside of you. Actually—maybe you get to *become* more abundant *because* of those moments. Maybe—I don't know how, but somehow?—maybe our hearts are made to be broken. Broken open. Broken free. Maybe the deepest wounds birth deepest wisdom.

We are made in the image of God. And wasn't God's heart made to be broken too? Wounds can be openings to the beauty in us. And our weaknesses can be a container for God's glory.

Hannah tasted salty tears of infertility. Elijah howled for God to take his life. David asked his soul a thousand times why it was so downcast. God does great things through the greatly wounded. God sees the broken as the best and He sees the best in the broken and He calls the wounded to be the world changers.

Up in the gable hangs the painting of Jesus breaking over all our brokenness, Jesus bleeding here in our chaos: *our bad brokenness is made whole by His good brokenness.*

If I could figure that out—live that out—then could I know the grace that knows how to live fully, even though you're brokenhearted?

The Farmer comes in from the barn, leaves a bucket from

the henhouse at the back door with his boots. I can hear him washing up at the mudroom's porcelain sink. He steps into the kitchen. I look up from the dishes. He's seen it already. The man can read my eyes better than he reads the skies. Sometimes all our unspoken broken speaks louder than anything we could ever say. He reads my slow breaking over the kid's lightning-bolt news and all my not-enoughness that I can't even grope through the pain to find words for.

He pulls me into himself, enfolds me. And then, into the quiet, he says it so soft I almost miss it, what I have held on to more than a thousand times since.

"You know—everything all across this farm says the same thing, you know that, right?" He waits till I let him look me in the eye, let him look into me and all this fracturing. "The seed breaks to give us the wheat. The soil breaks to give us the crop, the sky breaks to give us the rain, the wheat breaks to give us the bread. And the bread breaks to give us the feast. There was once even an alabaster jar that broke to give Him all the glory."

He looks right through the cracks of me. He smells of the barn and the dirt and the sky, and he's carrying something of the maple trees at the edge of the woods—carrying old light. He says it slowly, like he means it: "Never be afraid of being a broken thing."

I don't—I don't even know what that means. I *am* afraid. And I think this journey, this way, will not spare any of us. But maybe—this is the way to freedom? I've got to remember to just keep breathing—keep believing.

In Christ—no matter the way, the storm, the story—we always know the outcome.

Our Savior—surrounds.

Our future—secure.

Our joy—certain.

When we know Christ, we always know how things are going to go—always for our good and always for His glory.

Somehow Love can lodge light into wounds.

The warming spring sun falls behind him standing at the kitchen window. All across the field to the east, the wheat waves like a brazen promise.

I'll take it. I'll take his words like a daring covenant, not knowing yet what's to come: there is no growth without change, no change without surrender, no surrender without wound—no abundance without breaking. Wounds are what break open the soul to plant the seeds of a deeper growth.

My dad had told me this once. For a seed to come fully into its own, it must become wholly undone. The shell must break open, its insides must come out, and everything must change. If you didn't understand what life looks like, you might mistake it for complete destruction.

I whisper it to the Farmer, one line that unfolds like willing, cupped hands: "Brokenness can make abundance."

And the weight of hell shifts almost imperceptibly to feel more like the weight of glory, even if I'm not quite sure yet if that greater grace will come.

Two

Re-Membering Your Broken Pieces

But, first, remember, remember, remember . . .

C. S. LEWIS

The day after we'd held on to each other in the kitchen, this package came in the mail with three words—"Open Me Carefully"—as if it could be a soul.

I have no idea how this happens. How in the thick of ache you can be this solid dam—yet you catch bits of a song on a radio somewhere or the light falls a certain way across the floor or you lean the mailbox forward and a package slips right there into your hand—and in a moment, the loss of it all breaks you wide open.

Maybe it's because we never stop hoping for the best, waiting for the best like it got lost in the mail—and then one day there it is, unexpected and with our name right there on it.

I trace the ink across the top of the package—I don't recognize the handwriting.

The package is largish—and way too small for the shoulder-crushing load of questions about what the bloody point of all this is. I keep forgetting, me with the chronic soul amnesia.

A mourning dove coos out in the maple to the west of the kitchen. It calls out bravely, unafraid in its lament.

Hurt is a contagion. When one person hurts in a family, everyone aches. And this is always the choice: pain demands to be felt—or it will demand you feel nothing at all.

I slice the box open. Whatever it is, it's wrapped in tissue paper, a thin swaddling. I lift it from the box and this note falls to the table. It's from Peru, found in a shop that a friend was wandering through. She writes it across the embossed note-card: "Saw it and thought of you." The tissue paper feels like mummified dressings wrapped around something old enough to have the greatest story to tell. What do they say—that the great stories are the ones you need to hear again, the ones that call you back to find the wholeness of yourself again?

I unwrap slowly, hoping. There it is—something clay. Red clay. A base about eight inches long. Painted along its edge to look like thin bricks. Like a foundation, like the foundation for a story that might rejoin broken pieces. Unwrap it slowly, carefully—full of care for what might be. Thirteen small figures, earthen and primitive, kneel around the perimeter of the base, and it takes me a moment.

The Last Supper. The Great Story. A bent Jesus kneeling with His disciples, each of them kneeling before their own small cup and darkened loaf of bread.

This is the wholeness, right here in my hands, like my beginning and middle and end; this is the great story that defeats lostness and loneliness, that grows your heart larger. Maybe even large enough to break wide open.

There's something left in the box? Pieces roll around. And then I see the hand.

The hands of the Jesus are snapped right off. The Jesus has no hands.

I sit down. Jesus' hands lie there in front of Him, in front of all the disciples, two hands broken off, lying there palms open like an invitation.

The jug in front of Him is knocked over. Poured out.

How many times in your life do you get the Last Supper delivered to your very doorstep? Hadn't this been the story I'd been unpacking for the last five years? Hadn't I just been searching for an answer to the question of how to live with your one broken heart? Where is the abundant life? And how in the world to find it?

"And he took bread, gave thanks and broke it, and gave it to them . . ."[1]

I had first read it slowly, years ago—how in the original language "gave thanks" reads *eucharisteo*. The root word of *eucharisteo* is *charis*, meaning "grace." Jesus took the bread and saw it as grace and gave thanks.

There was more. *Eucharisteo*, thanksgiving, also holds the Greek word *chara*, meaning "joy." Joy. And that was what the quest for more has always been about—that which Augustine claimed, "Without exception . . . all try their hardest to reach the same goal, that is, joy."[2]

Deep *chara* is found only at the table of the *euCHARisteo*— the table of thanksgiving.

I had sat there long . . . wondering . . . is it that simple? *Is the height of my* chara *joy dependent on the depths of my* eucharisteo *thanks?*

So then as long as thanks was possible, then joy was always possible. The holy grail of joy was not in some exotic location or some emotional mountain peak experience. The joy wonder could be here, in the messy, piercing ache of now. The only place we need see before we die is this place of seeing God, *here and now.*

I'd whispered it out loud, let the tongue feel these sounds, the ear hear their truth.

Charis. Grace. *Eucharisteo*. Thanksgiving. *Chara*. Joy.[3]

A triplet of stars to reveal the outline of the fullest life, thanksgiving, joy. Five years of living thanks, of counting and giving thanks for one thousand everyday gifts, of struggling, miserably failing, and then purposing again to take everything as grace, gift—*charis*—give Him thanks for it—*eucharisteo*—and therein find joy in Him—*chara*.

But now, what of brokenness? And what did it mean that "bad brokenness is broken by good brokenness"? Had I only been scratching the surface? What if there was more to full abundance? And isn't the answer right here in my hands?

I hold the broken Last Supper in front of me, a Jesus with broken hands. What did Jesus do after He gave thanks?

"And he took bread, gave thanks and broke it, and gave it to them."[4]

He took it and gave thanks. Eucharisteo.

Then He broke it and gave.

How many times had I said it: "*Eucharisteo* precedes the miracle"? Thanksgiving precedes the miracle—the miracle of knowing all is enough. And how many times had I read it—how Jesus "took the seven loaves and the fish, and when he had given thanks, he broke them and gave them to the disciples, and they in turn to the people"?[5]

Eucharisteo—Jesus embracing and giving thanks for His not-enough—that preceded the miracle. But why hadn't I been awakened at the detonation of the revelation before? What was the actual miracle?

The miracle happens *in the breaking*.

Not enough was given thanks for, and then the miracle

happened: There was a breaking and a giving—into a kind of communion—into abundant filling within community. *The miracle happens in the breaking.*

I wonder if . . . if this is the truth that might make sense of so many questions—of all the pain? Not that I have any groping idea yet what that means—or what it will take to find out. But something about this unexpected moment, this gift, makes me want to try?

If *eucharisteo* had been the first dare, the first journey of discovery into a life of letting God love me and counting all those ways, could this be a dare for the next leg of the journey, the way leading higher up and deeper in, daring me to let all the not-enough there in my open hands—let it be broken into more than enough? A dare to let all my brokenness—be made into abundance. *Break and give away. The broken way.*

What if this were the safest embrace—the way of being wanted and held and found in the midst of falling apart? What did Jesus do? In His last hours, in His abandonment, Jesus doesn't look for comfort or try to shield Himself against the rejection; He breaks the temptation to self-protect—and gives the vulnerability of Himself. In the sharp edge of grief, Jesus doesn't look for something to fill the broken and alone places; He takes and gives thanks—and then does the most countercultural thing: He doesn't keep or hoard or hold on—but breaks and gives away. In the midst of intimate betrayal, He doesn't defend or drown Himself in addicting distractions; He breaks and is given—He gives His life. Because what else is life-giving?

Out of the fullness of the grace that He has received, He thanks, and breaks, and gives away—and He makes a way for life-giving communion. A broken way.

How does this make any rational sense? It doesn't. But

maybe that's the only way you ever know the greatest truths: The greatest truths always are the greatest paradox. And what could be a greater paradox than this? Out of feeling lavishly loved by God, one can break and give away that lavish love— and know the complete fullness of love.

The miracle happens in the breaking.

Somehow . . . the miracle of communion, oneness, wholeness, abundance, it happens in the exact opposite—in breaking and giving.

Somehow . . . the miracle, the intimacy, of communion comes through brokenness.

I run my fingers along the three cracks across the base of the sculpture.

What if a kind of communion is found in a trinity of brokenness—through broken places and broken people and being broken and given.

The hard clay feels like it's shaping something here in my hands. Like Someone is touching the rawness of the stinging wound.

When our own brokenness meets the brokenness of the world, don't we enter into and taste the brokenness and givenness of Christ?

And isn't this is the actual abundant wholeness of communion?

Somehow I wonder if it's in shattered places, with broken people, we are most near the broken heart of Christ. What if we only find our whole selves through this mystery—the mystery of death and resurrection, of brokenness and abundance? Could this be what it means to live in the encircling embrace of communion: brokenness giving way to abundance—and then abundance, which is then broken and given . . . gives way

"WHAT MATTERS IN LIFE

IS NOT WHAT HAPPENS TO YOU

BUT WHAT YOU REMEMBER

AND HOW YOU REMEMBER IT."

to an ever greater abundance? I think this—is the ring of the fellowship of communion. I move the broken pieces of the Last Supper closer together.

Why are we afraid of broken things? I can think of a thousand raw reasons. But touch the broken and the hungry and the hurting and the thirsty and the busted, and you touch a bit of Christ. *Why are we afraid of suffering?* What if the abundance of communion is only found there in the brokenness of suffering—because suffering is where God lives? Suffering is where God gives the most healing intimacy.

What if . . . what if I made a habit of every day pressing my wounds into the wounds of Christ—could my brokenness be made into a healing abundance for the brokenness of the world? A kind of communion? Could all brokenness meet in the mystery of Christ's brokenness and givenness and become the miracle of abundance? Wouldn't that be good brokenness breaking bad brokenness?

The strength of the reality weakens the knees here a bit. A paradigm shift—more like an earthquake, like a foundation is breaking. Breaking open.

Is this way realest life—or is life really this way? Am I saving myself . . . or dying—or both? Oh, God.

Picking up the broken hands of Jesus rolling about the cracked Last Supper, those two clay hands suddenly look like the offering of a gift, like an opening in the palm of my hand.

Jesus had said to do this in remembrance of Me—"to do," the Greek word *poieo*, a present imperative. The present tense indicates continuing action and can be translated "continue to do this." Continue to do this literally, with bread and wine—and continuously do this with your life, with the bread of your moments, the wine of your days.

A preacher's words had grabbed me by the lazy jugular: *This is the one and only command Christ gave to do continually over and over again.* This is the practice He gave for us to practice our faith, to practice again and again. *In remembrance of Him.* Continuously do this at the sink, at the stove, at the street corner, at the setting of the sun and at its rising again, and *never stop* continuously doing this.

Did I know anything about this? How was I doing the one command Christ asked to do continuously?

And continuously do what? Remember Me. We, the people with chronic soul amnesia, are called to be *the re-membering people.* The people who remember—and have their brokenness re-membered.

The shaft of light falling across the floor, falling across my feet—it's fractured by shadows from beyond the window.

Remembrance—it comes from the Greek word *anamnesis.*

The only four times this word *anamnesis* is used in Scripture, it is in reference to the sacrifice that Christ made and is "remembered" in the Last Supper (Luke 22:19; 1 Corinthians 11:24, 25; Hebrews 10:3).

The little clay-sculpted loaves in my hands feel like a memory I'm starved for. Like a memory become real between fingers.

I had read it once that *anamnesis* was a term used to express an intangible idea moving into this material, tangible world. The philosopher Plato had used the word *anamnesis* to express a remembering that allowed the world of ideas to impact the world of our everyday, allowing something in another world to take form in this physical one.

That was the point: remembrance, *anamnesis*, does not simply mean memory by mental recall, the way you remember your own address—but it means to experience a past event again through the physical, to make it take form through re-enactment. Like the way you remember your own grandma Ruth by how your great-aunt Lois laughs, how she makes butterscotch squares for Sunday afternoons too, how she walks in her Birkenstocks with that same soft heel as Grandma did, her knees cracking up the stairs the same way too. The way your great-aunt Lois acts makes you remember in ways that make your grandma Ruth real and physically present again now.

There's a cupping grace to it—how remembering becomes a healing. We welcome remembering, we hold remembering, we let remembering wrap around us and carry us like a dance that need not end.

We are never abandoned when we hold on to remembrance.

Gabriel García Márquez had scratched it down once, like words sealed in a bottle and sent back to the world: "What matters in life is not what happens to you but what you remember and how you remember it."[6]

That's it. What matters in your life is not so much what happens to you but what you happen to remember—and how that will influence how your life happens. What and how you remember will determine if your broken, dis-membered places will re-member you in your broken places.

So how to continuously re-member? Re-member your broken and busted heart, remember Him crucified and who you are and your real name: the Beloved.

"Continuously do *this* in remembrance of Me."

The truth of *anamnesis* is "to make Me [Christ] present." That's the truth of what He was saying: "Continuously make Me present." How in the world do you make Christ, who is always present, to be visibly present through this shattered chaos?

I turn the broken hands of Jesus over in mine. *Be broken and given in a thousand common and uncommon ways. Live given a thousand times a day. Die a thousand little deaths.* This feels like a dare that is choosing me. I don't know if I know how to do this. I don't know if I *want* to do this.

The sun pools. It's like the clay Jesus with no hands ignites mine with light.

The floor lights, everything lights: there is no physical body of Christ here on earth but ours. We are now Christ's only earthly body—and if we aren't the ones broken and given, we are the ones who dis-member Christ's body. Unless we are the ones broken and given, we incapacitate Christ's body on earth.

Maybe—there is no breaking of bad brokenness unless His people become good brokenness.

Something burns like a funeral pyre up my throat. What do I know about the Via Dolorosa? What do I know of this suffering and sacrifice of the broken way?

It's as though His broken hands beg me with a new begging dare.

Three

When You Want to Exchange Your Brokenness

The creation of the world seems to have been especially for this end, that the eternal Son of God might obtain a spouse towards whom he might fully exercise the infinite benevolence of his nature, and to whom he might, as it were, open and pour forth all that immense fountain of condescension, love, and grace that was in his heart.

JONATHAN EDWARDS

Our brazen hands reach out and take it every Sunday morning.

When they pass it from tired hand to hand in our country chapel on Sunday morning, when the ash-split basket with the loaf of bread that has just been broken in half passes from the gnarled hands of the hog farmer down to the wrinkled hands of the widow with her tarnished wedding band, still on to the mother reaching past the child sleeping open-mouthed on her lap, I watch. I watch how they press their fingers into the broken loaf, watch how we all tear into the loaf. We're all wolves in need of a lamb.

Do this in remembrance of Me. Continuously make the ever-present Christ present. Continuously be part of the re-membering of brokenness. This happens every Sunday. When you're a bloodied mess with that cursed chronic soul amnesia, it is good to remember your soul is dangerously emaciated for a reviving taste of His memory.

Mrs. Van Den Boogard passes the broken loaf to Mrs. Van Maneen. They tear off chunks of the loaf in hand, take crushed wheat to lips. And I'm rung loud: What in God's good and holy name are we all doing here? We ingest the broken. We become the broken. The wheat was crushed. Every kernel shattered for this bread. Every grape was crushed. The sweetness ran in the brokenness. *In shattered places, with broken people, we are most near the broken heart of Christ, and find our whole selves through the mystery of death and resurrection, through the mystery of brokenness and abundance.* We are the body sustained by His brokenness, His givenness, sustained by this Last Supper that for centuries was called simply "the thanksgiving"—the *eucharistias*.

That's the whole mess of us: the broken body comes to the thanksgiving to be fed the blessing of His broken and given body.

The miracle happens in the breaking—a breaking into the enoughness of communion.

The basket with the loaf moves to the end of my row, this movement of communion. They're passing it from hand to hand, closer. The piano is playing it like a stirring—"When I Survey the Wondrous Cross."

The miracle of intimate union, of communion, comes through brokenness—through broken places and broken people and the brokenness of Christ and being broken and given.

All throughout the sanctuary, there is the tearing of bread, the swallowing down.

This is how you live with your one broken heart: you give it away. This is how you enter into the wholeness of *koinonia*—communion.

The sanctuary cups a deepening stillness. An usher offers the bread across the aisle and gives it into willing hands. And I am imploding a bit, undone: No one is ever wholly fed—unless someone becomes a holy broken.

Oh, Jesus.

Out the country chapel windows all to the south, the fields of wheat wave in the wind. This bread and blood are symbols of His death—and they are the essence of our new life. Take it and taste it in a thousand ways: there is a revolution of brokenness turning right around into abundant wholeness right at the core of the universe.

All our brokenness meets in the mystery of Christ's brokenness and givenness—and becomes the miracle of abundance.

His words are the waving through wheat: "I say to you, unless a grain of wheat falls into the earth and dies, it remains alone; but if it dies, it bears much fruit."[1]

Death and resurrection. The paradox of it breaks into me afresh: unless we die, unless we surrender, unless we sacrifice, we remain alone. *Lonely.* But if we die, if we surrender, if we sacrifice, that is when we experience the abundance, that is when we dance in communion. The life that yields the most— yields the most.

The fields to the south sing in the surrender of it: "But if you let it go, reckless in your love, you'll have it forever, real and eternal."[2]

I've got to let it go. This bread, those crops, these people, everything.

And the Farmer hands me the basket of bread. What do

you do if you feel too wounded, too devastated to receive? Sometimes desperation drives you through devastation. I break off my piece of the loaf. *This is My body*—and the crushed kernels dissolve into me, become me. The wheat seed grew into a wheat stalk that ripened and was broken and came to my brokenness. If you didn't know how bread is made, you might think it looks like complete destruction.

Oh, Jesus.

Gary Goodkey, the pastor, hands the cup of the vine to Johnny Byles to pass down to the Farmer. And it's like the passing down of that story that knows your wounds and your name, and I swallow it down like a parched woman before the cup even gets to me.

It had been on the eve of Passover when I'd heard a pastor tell the story of how he'd been in Jerusalem, sitting in an Orthodox Jewish classroom, when a Jewish rabbi started teaching the marriage customs of first-century Jews.

He'd up and said that when a man had decided whom he'd chosen to marry, his father would pour a cup of wine and pass it down to his son. The son would then turn to the young woman he loved, and with all the solemnity of an oath before Almighty YHWH Himself, the young man would hold out the cup of wine to the woman and ask for her hand in marriage. He would ask with these words: "This cup is a new covenant in my blood, which I offer to you."

The pastor had told me how he'd sat back, a bit stunned. This Orthodox Jewish rabbi was describing first-century marriage customs, a marriage proposal—with the words Jesus had used that night: "This cup is the new covenant in my blood, which I offer to you."

The Last Supper was a marriage covenant.

IN SHATTERED PLACES,

WITH BROKEN PEOPLE,

WE ARE MOST NEAR

THE BROKEN HEART OF CHRIST.

I feel too broken to be chosen.

Then the pastor had said it slowly so it couldn't be missed, cup outstretched in his hands: "In other words, Jesus says to you with this cup, 'I love you. I want you. I covenant Myself to you. I commit to you. This cup is the new covenant in My blood, which I offer to you. *Do you love Me? Will you covenant yourself to Me?*'"

It's happening right now. The cup passes from Claude to Harold to Mary. This is what's happening—that truth a preacher once shared with me: every Communion service is a remembrance of the intimate marital act. Both the Communion service and the intimate marital act are nothing less than a covenant renewal ceremony.[3]

I take the cup of red with a shaky hand on Sunday morning. Who takes the dare to their lips? Who seals their yes with a kiss? Can you believe that in all your broken, you can still be chosen? That you are?

Will you make a commitment to Me like I have made to you?

Every abandonment ever experienced could be abandoned in this sacramental act. Will I take the cup of His heart? If I take it, if I drink it, I accept His life for mine. And I offer Him mine.

And I become the failure breaking. I am the woman with secrets she doesn't know how to speak, with sins that are like hidden black mold growing up the side of her soul, who's ached with a silent suffering and felt shattered at the base of her crumbling foundations and knows what it means to be lost, not quite knowing how to rebuild. I'm the woman whose machete tongue has torn a strip off her kids' backsides, the friend who has slapped up cold, guarded walls to protect her heart at the cost of anyone else's heart, the woman who's been more interested in self-preservation than anyone else's situation. I'm the mom whose kid seems bent a bit on self-destruction right now, who can't stop her torrid affair with guilt, the wife whose neck can stiffen like an unwilling pillar of salt, who has fallen and broken herself and is desperate for Someone to put her back together again. I am the failure breaking—and they hand me the cup of crushed fruit of the vine. If I take it, if I drink it, I accept His life. And I offer Him mine.

"By the wedding ring of faith, He shares in the sins, death, and pains of hell which are His bride's," Martin Luther wrote as his very first image to explain the good news of the gospel. "As a matter of fact, [Christ] makes [our sins] His own," he wrote, his pen on fire: "Here this rich and divine bridegroom Christ marries this poor, wicked harlot, redeems her from all her evil, and adorns her with all His goodness. Her sins cannot now destroy her, since they are laid upon Christ and swallowed up by Him."[4]

Who has ever loved you to death like this?

And I tilt my head back and swallow down the bloody red of the vine and my sins are swallowed up by Him. And then the relief of it comes, this is the otherworldly union: "Faith . . . unites the soul with Christ as a bride is united with her bridegroom."[5] Luther's words touch all these sharp places within.

> From such a marriage, as St. Paul says, it follows that Christ and the soul become one body—so that they hold all things in common, whether for better or worse. This means that what Christ possesses belongs to the believing soul, and what the soul possesses belongs to Christ . . . Christ possesses all good things and holiness; these now belong to the soul. The soul possesses lots of vices and sin; these now belong to

Christ . . . Christ, the rich, noble, and holy bridegroom, takes in marriage this poor, contemptible, and sinful little prostitute, takes away all her evil, and bestows all His goodness upon her! It is no longer possible for sin to overwhelm her, for she is now found in Christ.[6]

Found—in Christ.

I want to grab all those polite Communion cups and swig down the whole paltry tray. I want to stand up in a stilled sanctuary, stand on my seat, and shout yes, a thousand yeses—I will take Him because He takes even me, even me. *Could He take me?*

"Who then can fully appreciate what this royal marriage means?" Luther begs the believer to take hold of the incomprehensible: "Who can understand the riches of the glory of this grace? . . . And she has that righteousness in Christ, her husband—of which she may boast as of her own and which she can confidently display alongside her sins in the face of death and hell and say, 'If I have sinned, yet my Christ, in whom I believe, has not sinned, and all His is mine and all mine is His.'"[7]

How can it be? When we're naked and ashamed and alone in our brokenness, Christ envelops us with His intimate grace. When we're rejected and abandoned and feel beyond wanting, Jesus cups our face: "Come close, my Beloved." When we're dirty and tear-stained and despairing, Jesus Christ is attracted to us and proposes undying love: "All that you're carrying I take . . . and all that I am is yours."

How do you ever get over that? "For this movement is like the approach of a bridegroom to the bride. Its proper consummation like the giving and receiving of a ring in marriage. Indeed, it is like the crowning intercourse of love itself."[8] There is a kind of intimacy that can only be tasted and swallowed. There is a wooing that washes your wounds. There is a union for all this brokenness.

"Ultimately it comes down to this, that the real cause of our trouble is failure to realize our union with Christ," Martyn Lloyd-Jones wrote.[9] That. I sit there in the realization of that real cause of all troubles.

A hush settles over the sanctuary.

All our brokenness is only healed by union.

Isn't this what I'd known in a museum in Paris, what I'd discovered of union in the counting of one thousand gifts of His love?

The pieces of me, the shards I didn't know how to gather together again, the ache that kept me up at night that I didn't even have words for—none of the pieces of me would find peace—until I could see and feel and experientially enter into the reality of my union with Christ. Peace isn't a place—it's a Person. Peace isn't a place to arrive at, but a Person to abide in. "I myself am your peace," says Jesus.[10]

Is this how you live with your one broken heart? Your one broken heart is only healed by a oneness with Him.

Am I willing to give all that I have to Him? And God forbid—what if He hadn't given me all that He is?

I look across the sanctuary to the passing of broken bread, crushed grapes, down the rows of open hands, across the aisles. This is what this all is: communion with Him is not simple symbolism; it is utter radicalism. Can I incarnate being broken and given in thanks to Christ? I can still taste the sweet brokenness of the grain and the grape in the back of my mouth. My mind's spinning, wrapping around what is happening here: the Last Supper embodies the fullest DNA of the body of Christ, of the church. Giving thanks—then breaking and giving. The doxology, then discipleship. The *eucharisteo*, then *koinonia*.

Koinonia—I'd understood it only as communion, as fellowship, but it's so much more, no less than full participation in Christ's brokenness and givenness, a deeper union with Him. I feel it now: *koinonia* is no mere symbol, but this miraculous embrace that can end our abandonment, our aloneness. It's this enveloping relationship of the outstretched cross, sharing in the oneness of the very life of Christ. And isn't the very essence of the church this willing *koinonia*, the intimate union between God and humanity, the gift that both comes from God and is the goal of God?

There's a thrumming across the sanctuary, across the whole universe: we aren't merely called to get to know Christ; we are called to participate in complete union with Christ. He breaks and gives His life to the broken. And in communion—*koinonia*—the broken get to live given to Him, the God who sought intimate *koinonia* walking in the garden with Adam, who pursued a close communing with Enoch, who spoke face-to-face with Moses, as a man speaks to his closest friend. Communion is always more than an intimate service; it's ultimately being given in intimate service to Him. We are made partakers (*koinonia*) of Christ and the divine nature,[11] and He comes in a radical act of *koinonia* and makes His home tending to our aching places.[12] There's this pulsing through my surrendered wounds: "You, God, are my God, earnestly I seek you. I thirst for you, my whole being longs for you, in a dry and parched land where there is no water."[13]

Can I remember? Can I enter into the radical discipleship and radical symbolism of the Last Supper and find what I've wanted since the beginning—communion . . . *koinonia* . . . the oneness that heals my one broken heart?

That's what the call is, that's what is reverberating in the space between the pews and all our souls: be the remembering people.

I wonder if all the bad brokenness in the world begins with the act of forgetting—forgetting God is enough, forgetting what He gives is good enough, forgetting there's always more than enough and that we can live into an intimate communion. Forgetting is kin to fear.

Whenever I forget, fear walks in. *We're called to be a people known by our remembering—a remembering people.* Forget to give thanks—and you forget who God is. Forget to break and give—and it's your soul that gets broken. Forget to live into *koinonia*, into communion—and you end up living into a union of emptiness.

If all our bad brokenness begins with an act of forgetting, then doesn't the act of remembering, then making Christ present by being broken and given, doesn't that lead to *koinonia*, communion, which literally re-members us?

Everything He embodied in the Last Supper—it is what would heal the body's brokenness. Brokenness can be healed in re-membering. Remembering our union, our communion, our *koinonia*, with Christ. Re-membering heals brokenness.

I never want to stop tasting the broken grain and the grape there at the back of my longing throat.

That is why we're called to be *the re-membering people*—remembering the heart of God for us, remembering the cross and the communion and the crucifixion, remembering the *koinonia*, remembering to be broken and given into the world—so Jesus can re-member all our broken hearts.

Because when we who are broken give to the broken—this is giving ourselves to Him, the Wounded Healer, the Broken and Given Lover. And He gives us His open and given heart, gives us His very life, gives us union . . . communion. Was this the essence of Christianity? Not only giving thanks—but giving ourselves to Him in a thousand ways and faces? I can't stop answering His proposal with an unlikely yes—yes. *I take You—and You take me.* All I have, for all of Him.

On the way home, all this light that we can feel, it gets in along all the cracks.

When we walk in the back door from Sunday service, from the breaking of bread and thick intimacy of exchange, there's this black pen lying on the table across from the broken Peruvian Lord's Supper.

I pick up the pen and turn my wrist over. How many years had I cut that paling wrist, wearing my brokenness on the outside? I pick up the pen, and on a whim—on a conviction, kind of ridiculously desperate to remember the radical symbolism, to remember the union, the communion—I write it on my wrist, let it bleed like a vow right there into the thin white skin: one little black cross.

I am busted and His, and He is broken and given and mine.

I trace that one black cross: *Can you dare to break yourself into a kind of communion, a kind of union? Can you let the way be made for broken places to re-member?*

It's like this is one wild dare to live cruciform, to let life become shaped like a cross. This could be a dare to let life be shaped like union.

It's a dare to be married to mysteries so Christ has hands again in this world—and specifically mine.

The broken hands of Jesus lie there on the buffet, beside the little clay Lord's Supper. I turn them over. His hands in mine, my hands for His. My wrist penned with His cross. There's more than a thousand ways for Christ to have hands in a busted world so the brokenhearted can find a deeper kind of whole.

The clouds have broken. Broken open to the west now. It's raining slow—like a letting go into the *more* you can almost believe will come.

Four

How to Break
Time in Two

As if you could kill time without injuring eternity.
HENRY DAVID THOREAU

When I wake up the morning of my fortieth birthday, I couldn't care a rat's bony hind leg if the sun ever shows its face again, or if there's a half-price sale on boots down at The Bay or if I ever get to trek through Iceland or if the kids pick up whatever's exploded like volcanic debris all over the house. You can forget there's any light in living, in your soul. You can find it hard to remember. Your pen can run out of blue ink and you can lose that gratitude journal and ask me how I know. I can get God-Alzheimer's.

I roll over, bury my head under the pillow. Anxiety can come out of nowhere. Get busy, get distracted, and you can forget God. Forget God, and you lose your mind and your peace. Forget God, and all you remember is anxiety. Anxiety can give you God-Alzheimer's. Forget the face of God, and you forget your own name is Beloved. *Beloved, you are the re-membering people. Find your feet. Find His face—His broken-wide-open heart of communion.*

I lie there for what feels long, and not nearly long enough.

The hands of the clock on the wall, they keep following the invisible, trying to track it.

I can hear the dog slurping from that one-handled pot we demoted to a water dish.

A cousin, she'd called at midnight. We've got whole yellowing photo albums of us with big bangs and pop-bottle glasses. Her third-year university son who'd been baptized and shared his testimony before the whole congregation, he'd just decided he's actually an atheist. He's done with the supposed flimsy fairy tales. You can howl with a mother at midnight and feel the weight of darkness filling your moans.

My ninth-grade science teacher, Mr. Biesel, said you can't see time. Time can only be represented by change, by the way things move and change. I lie there on a birthday morning, not wanting to get out of bed, as if I can change, and still stop time. Middle-age birthdays and—oh, how did it all become so late so soon? *Is anything you're doing here adding up to anything that matters? And in the end, is what you've chosen ultimately about Christ and His kingdom?* If not, then no matter what you've chosen, it won't matter at all.

That cross I'd penned onto my wrist the day before, it's about rubbed off. I've got no bloody idea at all how you take this dare. How can all the bad brokenness be broken with good brokenness? How do you live cruciform—and be broken and given into a kind of communion?

There's a mama round the corner from the farm, they say she's been up for days rocking that brand-new daughter of hers who the doctors conceded last week has a fatal disease. What in God's good name was the clock on her wall saying?

I'd sat up late the night before to write back to my friend Elizabeth. We had met nearly six years ago—two mothers with nearly a dozen kids between the two of us—commiserating over houses that seemed to manufacture chaos like it was our actual business plan. I told her I was trying to remember to put my priorities on all things unseen. Told her I was trying to slay the idol of the seen, break the idols of performance, and believe the state of my house doesn't reflect the state of my soul. And she'd confirmed it's the priorities unseen—the prayers, the relationships, the love while doing the work—that hold the meaning, the merit. And she'd leaned in and asked if we could be friends for life, and I had said, "Deal," and laughed way too loud.

I couldn't have known then that Elizabeth would turn out to be unlike any other friend I'd ever had. Who else sends courage in a box and pounds of milk chocolate that would show up at the door? Who else would reach out late at night and say, "I see you, the you behind everything you're doing, and I like you—the you that just is"? Who else lived out priorities unseen—priorities that let the people around her, me, be known? I couldn't have known then that Elizabeth would be the friend for life that my life needed in ways I hadn't expected.

Then last night, Elizabeth said hospice had just started coming to the house.

How do you end up being forty-something with hospice knocking on your front door? How can God let the world break a bit like this? How is *this* all grace? How is *this* love?

I bury my head deeper into the pillow. Rub a bit at that smudged cross on my wrist . . . and yet *it is love. Who knows why God allows heartbreak, but the answer must be important enough because God allows His heart to break too.*

I reach for the pen on my nightstand, the way I've reached for ink to count a thousand ways He loves me, the way ink's been the cheapest of medicines. But now—can the ink be lived, branded onto the skin, how could it leave the page and lead a way through pain? The ink would start right there on my scarred wrist, right where part of me wanted to kind of die, and not in the saving way, and somehow there is good brokenness that grows out of every scar and wound we will ever suffer. *Draw one line vertically down my wrist, right over scars.* The question of evil and suffering is answered in the breaking of God's own heart too. *Draw another line horizontally across my wrist, breaking scar lines with cross lines.* Our broken hearts always break His. It's the quantum physics of God: Your one broken heart always splits God's heart in two. You never cry alone.

And still—your brokenness can feel like a tomb you can't quite claw yourself out of. Is the most painful kind of tears the kind no one can see, the kind where your soul weeps alone? You can feel the corners and edges of you withering with the weight of scar tissue on your own soul.

The flannel sheets feel like grave clothes. *How long can I refuse to move?* Exhale.

Maybe air isn't all that keeps you alive. There's a cross that's helping me breathe. It's reminding me, re-forming me, and I'm so insufferably forgetful. I try to remember that grace swallowed with courage is elemental to living.

Inked cross bleeding into my arms. Swallow down His grace. What He gives is enough—enough courage to move up out of bed. *One small step for a woman, one giant leap for her sanity.* The woman with broken kids, the friend with dying friends, the ache of a broken heart. Just take the first step. And then the next step. Courage is reaching out and taking just a bit of that iron-nail grace.

I make my hand reach out, the one with that penned cross,

make that hand reach out and turn on the light. The way you always find the light in the dark is to make your hand reach out.

Find an old flannel shirt in the bottom dresser drawer, pull on the worn threads over outstretched arms. So if we're all born with our hands clenched into these tight fists—what does it mean to live with hands wide open, hands reached out?

How in the world will you live with your one broken heart?

A book sits in a pond of light on the edge of the dresser. In the kitchen, a crumbling handful of yesterday's cookies sits on a plate. When I wander out to the red mailbox at the end of our lane, I leave a book and brown paper bag of cookies for the mail carrier.

On the way in, I will myself to pick a bunch of zinnias and glads from the weedy, tangled patch masquerading as a garden. I say their name out loud as I pick—"glads, glads, glads." *Remind me. Rewire me.* That cross on my wrist begs like a prayer:

Become cruciform. Like a cross. Transform.

If it is true that to become cruciform, to let your life become shaped like a cross, is to become more fully human—and most fully like Christ—then this is the work most urgent, most needed.

The dirt in the garden feels like gritty grace there underneath fingernails. I've got no idea what made me think of taking these flowers to the nursing home in town right then, and there isn't a bone in my weary body that wants to do it. There are days you don't want to keep breathing—but your body doesn't forget how and it does it anyway.

Your body breathes for you anyway. And you are part of a body always. There's a cross that is your backbone, and all you have to do is reach out your arms.

Find water for the zinnias. Reach for the Mason jars for vases. The way to find the light in the dark is to make your hand reach out—reach out in thanks, reach out in giving. And maybe your hand has to reach out so your heart keeps beating—so someone else keeps breathing. Maybe this can be a way to keep breaking the bread and reaching out to pass it down, right through brokenness.

How can I not keep reaching out while I'm still alive?

Maybe because the clock was ticking loud while I filled those Mason jars, maybe that's what made me think of how I wanted to spend my fortieth birthday. Or maybe it was the filling of the Mason jars. Maybe because it *was* my birthday and I could choose what I wanted, and what I wanted was to not waste any more of time that keeps running through my fingers like water. Maybe because I'd thought of what Elizabeth with her terminal cancer had told me. I'd looked right into the watery hope of her eyes when she said that whenever she met with her doctor in that sterile white room, what she wanted most was a number. What all terminal patients really want is a number.

"How long have I got, Doc?"

Elizabeth had said it directly, like she wanted to lodge it squarely into me. "The real wrestling in living and in dying is always a wrestle for a number."

My Elizabeth was dying, and she still hadn't any idea how much time she actually had to live. Maybe knowing you're dying changes everything—*while actually changing nothing.* Because we all know it every single day, whether we have a diagnosis or not: we all get one container of time—but no one gets to know what size that container is.

There are only so many full orbits around the sun, and who makes time to lie in bed and listen to rain thrumming on roofs or to take someone for strawberry ice cream sundaes and linger down at the bridge, the river running underneath like the present running through your hands. And there are glads to be picked from the earth and there is time yet to live in the givenness of everything.

Your time is limited—so don't limit your life by wanting someone else's.

Sometimes I stand in the living room after they're all in bed, and listen to that clock tick slowly. Sometimes the ticking of the clock is like Morse code, tapping it out again and again:

You have only one decision every day: how will you use your time?

Sometimes the best use of your time is to stand and listen to a clock. We're all terminal—and we all just want a number. *What size is this bucket of time? How many days do I actually get?*

Back when the calendar flung itself into a new year, our youngest one with the sprinkle of freckles across her nose asked me how many days a person gets to live, and I didn't know what to say. I'd told her that maybe, maybe her number was 25,550?

How do you tell a child that time is a vapor and that even if you reach your hand out, it will run through like water and fall like dew and soon will all be gone?

Shalom had laughed like a hoot owl, rolled across the white quilt of my bed. "You're making it up now, Mama."

"I ain't." I yanked one of her curled bare toes. She felt like tangle-headed adventures and sticky buns on Saturday mornings and the creek rising in the back woods and unbridled hope—an unfurling. She felt like time embraced. "Why would your crazy old mama make up a number like that?"

Her freckles had crinkled. "She would!"

"Well, if you get seventy years—*if*—then from the day you're born till you fly away Home, you'd get 25,550 days. That's your number, girl—maybe."

God, give us whole buckets of time. And "the man who would know God must give time to Him."[1] It's like the cross penned into skin is silently pleading.

Shalom sat up on the bed, like she'd seen something. Like she needed to understand it.

She pulls her knees up to her chin. "What's a number like that look like?"

"It looks like . . ."

Time looks like light caught in the limbs of willing trees, I think, like laugh lines bracketing a thousand brave smiles, like a steady current of wrinkled sheets and slow dawns, of steam rising off bowls, of opening and closing back doors and the click of thousands of last lights out. Time is always a stream of God's "unbounded Now," C. S. Lewis wrote.[2] *It looks like a river of Nows. Unbounded. Broken free.*

"You know . . ." I sink down beside her. "Your dad plants one and a half million kernels of wheat an acre out there every spring." Looking out the window to the east, the wheat moves like a rising from beyond, cresting up over the hills. "And those one and a half million kernels work out to about two bushels of wheat. So 25,550 kernels is . . . pretty much about four cups of wheat."

I look her squarely in the eye. "Go get a glass jar."

She slides off the bed, eyes watching mine. She finds an old blue Mason jar with wavy, bubbled glass and hands it to me. It's smooth and sure in my palm. I turn it over. A jar in my hands. A cross written over the scars on my wrist. Hauling out the large bag of wheat used to make bread, I stand in front of the pantry and measure out four cups of kernels.

We pour them, careful not to drop the jar.

"There's your 25,550 days," I say.

Our girl rolls the jar between her hands. *There's your life,* I think. *How will you live with your one broken heart?* The kernels of wheat rain against the glass. Take your one container of time and believe it contains exactly the time you need for a meaningful life.

"How many kernels do I have to take out?" she whispers. "The ones that are already gone for me, that I've already lived."

That are already gone.

She holds the jar up to the light, liquefying it into gold. "How many kernels do you have left? Half of this?" She had turned, and the sun from across the cosmos lit her hair. She's quiet, rolling the jar. I can hardly hear her whisper: "I don't want to think about that." But she can't stop: "Do you have just half a jar left?" No one can measure the length of your life, but you can always determine that your life has meaning. She'd murmured it like we were in a holy place: "All we are . . . are these grain days."

These grain days. These grace days.

All I can think is, *"Unless a grain of wheat falls into the earth and dies, it remains alone; but if it dies, it bears much fruit."*[3]

There's a way to multiply your life. You let every kernel die.

"Be cruciform—like I am cruciform."

I don't think I'd noticed it before, how the hands on the clock keep reaching out.

Shalom keeps rolling the jar. And I stop it. *Try to make everything stop.* And I hold the jar, lifting it again up to the light.

I wonder if I've had this all wrong. When I've thought of

time, I've thought of it as something to seize, to try to capture, or that's captured and stolen from us, and I'd try to slow it down before it steals away. I've thought of time as something you have to wring the very most out of, drain to the last drop. *Carpe diem, people, carpe diem.*

But what had Jesus said? "My time has come."[4] What time? The time *of His death*? For Jesus, time was not something you seize as much as something you sacrifice. How had I always, all my life, thought of time as this highway robber that *steals* life, until we ultimately die? But all through Scripture, Jesus speaks of time as the *highway* by which we have come to die—so we can ultimately *get to* more abundant life. Time isn't something you seize; it's something you sacrifice. It's not something to grab; it's something to *give*.

If *eucharisteo*, giving thanks, slows down time . . . then can being broken and given in communion break time by actually multiplying it? Maybe time gets broken and multiplied and made into something more whenever someone breaks and gives herself or himself away.

Death stops time for us here and makes us a seed to be buried in the ground—but maybe when we die to self, we break time here and our sacrificial love breaks into eternity, going on forever. "Love never dies."[5] Isn't that exactly what Jesus did to break time's death grip on us? He died, and His death broke a hole in the wall of time and abundant life without became a possible new door for all of us to escape out of time.

Maybe temporary time is made for dying to self—so your eternal self can really live.

Have the hands of the clock stopped moving there in the kitchen? It takes courage to listen with our whole heart to the tick of God's timing rather than march to the loud beat of our fears.

Time can't dictate dreams or hijack hope or determine destination. It can't force us into living anything but what we believe. No matter what the hands of the clock say, underneath us all are the everlasting arms, and time's arms are too weak to rob any hope, steal any prayers, destroy any joy, or crush any purpose. Time never heals wounds like God does.

It's God hands that control the universe. The hands of the clock are bound by the decisions of our hands. And He has made our hands free to be His.

I'd turned the transparent, vulnerable jar of wheat round, tried to count grains, envisioned each of those kernels as days, the only time I have. It's a *jarring* thought. *The way to break time's hold on me is to be broken and given with my time.*

There was a stray kernel on the counter, another left in the measuring cup. I picked up each gold nugget with the tip of my finger. *You can't waste one.* You can't afford not to break each grain day—*die to self*—and have twice as much life. *Wasn't the cross on my wrist daring just that?*

The shape of multiplied time looks like a cross. Cruciform. Broken and given, reaching right out.

There's enough time yet for picking glads in muggy August morning sunshine and filling Mason jar vases of blooms for sidelined, forgotten people. There's time for lingering over cups of coffee and listening to the pouring out of someone's cracked heart, time for long phone calls and shared pie and going the extra mile. And there's time to be broken and given into all the world's brokenness, because this is how to break time's hold.

At the beginning of the year, I'd left the lid off the Mason jar, watched Shalom run her hand again and again through the kernels.

Maybe what matters isn't what we want from the time we have to live . . . but what time wants from us.

Why is it so easy to kill time instead of using time to die to self and feel a resurrection?

The gladiolas lie on the counter, waiting for a container.

Five

Becoming the Gift the World Needs—and You Need

It is beyond the realm of possibilities that one has the ability to out give God. Even if I give the whole of my worth to Him, He will find a way to give back to me much more than I gave.

CHARLES SPURGEON

A hunching giant of a man who now lives in Room 112 at the nursing home in town, he had prayed for our boys every day. He'd shown me their names scrawled on his list and said it like an answer to prayer. "Never live for battles won or for the end of your run. What matters is how you live in 'the along.' And it's there in the along that you have to remember: people care more what you share with them than what you ever say to them."

I grab that tin bucket the Farmer left on the top step at the back door. I pour every single one of the 25,550 wheat kernels out of that dusty Mason jar that's been sitting up there on the windowsill since the beginning of the year, looking like a time capsule. Like a dare to break time.

I fill it with water and glads and schlepp a bunch of those jar vases over to the nursing home. The kids and I leave them in the doorways of the residents' rooms, and there's no missing the beauty of what these have held and what they're containers for now—or how entire wings of the nursing home light up in these thousand-watt smiles. On hard days of wrestling with time and pieces of your broken past, turns out you can always find a way to reach out your hand and just turn the light on.

When we're standing in Room 112 with Mr. Bender, he leans worn and tall over us and asks us to sing one more hymn, and I choke it back a bit when he says right at the end, just before we leave that Mason jar of glads with him, "Promise you won't shed a tear when I finally come to the end of my run and I'm not here but have up and gone? You'll know I am finally home with my God."

Koinonia, communion.

The soul craves more than only communication; it seeks communion. Is the most authentic communication always a kind of communion, a breaking and giving into oneness, into love?

Mr. Bender reaches over and squeezes my hand and nods, and time divides and flies. Someday Mr. Bender will. It begins right there and I can feel it: something that's been broken in you . . . can start to break.

Let it come. Let it come.

I don't think I know quite what that could mean.

Leaving the nursing home, we pass the police car on Main Street in front of Chocolates on Main, and those crazy boys of ours want to leave a box of cookies there on the hood of a sunning cruiser. They have no shame in saying a little too loudly the box may be mistaken for a bomb.

It's all like a slow match in me that could start an explosion. Could there be a better way to spend time and find the meaning of being and celebrate another birthday, than to break through the anxiety that keeps a life bound and small? What if it detonated in my own heart: reach out your one weak arm and let your own brokenness start to mend and touch the heat of communion? *Can I trust that He's enough in me to make me enough?* This is all part of the figuring, the finding of the way.

The measure of your willingness to be given—is the measure of your capacity for communion.

We grab a pie at Zehrs Markets and drop it off at our doctor's office and thank him for catching babies. We head to the local coffee shop and pay for a line of coffees behind us (*"Yes, really. Yes, we're serious. Yes, for real!"*). We grab a dozen donuts to deliver to the fine folks at the town office.

And there's this moment, a glance catching my reflection in the coffee shop window, and this grinning, birthing thought: *learning the art of living is learning the art of giving.*

For God so loved that *He gave . . .*[1]

The art of giving is believing there is enough love in you, that you are loved enough by Him, to be made enough love to give.

For God so loved that He gave . . . Is there any word more powerful than *giving*? *Thanksgiving. Forgiving. Care-giving. Life-giving.* Everything that matters in living comes down to giving.

"Giving is true having," is what Spurgeon said.[2] There's the whole street looking back at me in the window's reflection. What if there are times you have to look back in order to understand the things that lie ahead?

The love of God always gives, always breaks itself and

gives—*to give joy.* God seeks His own glory only because He vows that He is the God who gives—gives what we need most.

There's an ache in me that needed all this. Like it's the beginning, the way, to something more.

For a string of thirty days, as part of this dangerous dare, we'd read it aloud as a family after the evening meal, read God's beckoning words:

> "What I'm interested in seeing you do is: sharing your food with the hungry, inviting the homeless poor into your homes, putting clothes on the shivering ill-clad, being available to your own families. Do this and the lights will turn on, and your lives will turn around at once. Your righteousness will pave your way. The GOD of glory will secure your passage. Then when you pray, GOD will answer. You'll call out for help and I'll say, 'Here I am.'"[3]

There are lights turning on, all down the street. I can feel things inside, broken things, turning around, a passage being paved through Him. A way.

"Do you hesitate, man, to go this way, when this is the way that God came to you?" Augustine murmurs from the edges of things.[4] Something's happening in the giving . . .

The police officer's chuckling over his box of cookies.

God is most glorified in us when we are most enjoying Him—*and giving others the joy of Him.*

And I want to reach out and cup the face of that birthday girl staring back at me in the coffee shop window and convince her: there is no life worth living without generosity because generosity is a function of abundance mentality. And abundance mentality is a function of identity and intimacy. When you know you are loved enough, that you are made enough, you have abundantly enough to generously give enough. And that moves you into the enoughness of an even more intimate communion.

I think maybe this is touching the edge of the true nature of the dare?

It's like an enfolding ring: it's the presence of Christ who gives us every single gift. And the presence of Christ makes us into the gift given. There are no gifts in the world, given or received, without the presence of Christ. Christ gives the gifts to us, and then—He within us, indwelling us—He gives the gifts through us to a beautiful and aching world.

Bread broken and given, shared.

"He broke it and gave it . . . The bread which we break, is it not the *koinonia*, the communion, of the body of Christ?"[5]

What we break and give comes back to us as a bit of communion. *Koinonia*, a soul sharing, a givenness, a participation. The very moment of my *salvation* in Christ made my *union* with Christ an objective *fact*, but it's not until this moment of realization of *communion* with Christ that there's *experiential* joy.

This is a sort of communion.

When you walk into a diner across the street and tell the waitress you're paying for that family's dinner, it's a thing you don't forget, and it feels like an act of re-membering. The waitress laughs and you wink and leave before they're finished at the all-you-can-eat buffet. A diner and hungry people and the presence of Christ in you, reaching your unsure hand out, can taste like a sacrament.

Live eucharist. Practice communion. Taste *koinonia*. Feel abundant life. All I can think is this: *this is how you make the ever-present Christ fully present.* This is the beginning of becoming the gift. Allow Christ in you to give away the gift of Himself right through your brokenness. God gives God so we can be the givers. The gift-ers.

This truth of "the blessedness of possessing nothing" and all such truths, writes Tozer, "can not be learned by rote as one would learn the facts of physical science. They must be *experienced* before we can really know them . . . If we would indeed know God in growing intimacy we must go this way of renunciation. And if we are set upon the pursuit of God, He will sooner or later bring us to this test."[6]

Being in pursuit of Him as He relentlessly pursues me in this growing intimacy had brought me sooner or later to this, this dare to live the communion of living the shape of the cross, living cruciform.

The boys gift the tennis court with a whole bunch of tennis balls ("Don't you think some kids are gonna be surprised, Mom?"). And I slip into the back door of the library, leave a few of my favorite books at the desk; then the whole lot of us circle over to the grocery store on Mitchell Street, put away grocery carts, grab a few bags of groceries, and drop them off at the food bank. Stick quarters into bubble gum machines at Walmart. Scope out the grocery store to buy a cart of groceries for someone. Tuck parking fees into envelopes, and slide them under windshield wipers for those in the hospital parking lot.

The Farmer winks at me and laughs, stuffing envelopes. "You know what? We've got time for this."

I nod, wink back. Time is made for dying in a thousand ways, so why be afraid of dying when a kind of dying could come all the time? Live every day like you're terminal. Because you are. Live every day like your soul's eternal. *Because it is.*

MAYBE THE ONLY

ABUNDANT WAY FORWARD

IS ALWAYS

TO GIVE FORWARD.

And, obviously, we can't pay the cosmos back. So maybe we forget about paying it forward? We can only *give* it forward. Give It Forward Today. Be the GIFT. Give *Him*. Maybe the only abundant way forward is always to give forward.

I don't even know who has the audacious idea to go up to the dollar store and leave dollars up and down every aisle, but our kids watch unsuspecting kids wander in. Smiles break up every aisle. And maybe a bit of the world's brokenness breaks by this good brokenness.

This boy in a ball cap stops at the counter and picks up a lollipop we've taped a note to: "Here's a dollar. Pick any color. We're Giving It Forward Today. #BeTheGift." His face explodes in this smile, and bits of joy lodge in the brokenness of me and I feel a bit remade.

Smiling at anyone is to awe at the face of God. And "the beauty of the world is Christ's tender smile coming to us through matter."[7] There's a clerk grinning at the till. The guy stocking shelves is chuckling. There are people Giving It Forward Today, and don't think that every gift of grace, every act of kindness, isn't a quake in a heart that moves another heart to give, that moves another heart to give, that grows into an avalanche of grace. Don't say this isn't what a brokenhearted world desperately needs, don't say it isn't how to change a broken world. What if the truth really is that every tremor of kindness here erupts in a miracle elsewhere in the world?

I can feel it like the slightest sense of a suturing along raw and ragged scar lines. Maybe our suffering and brokenness begin a kind of healing when we enter into the suffering and brokenness of the world, right through the brokenness and givenness of Christ.

And these acts of kindness, gifts of grace, they start a

cascade of grace to fill a multitude of canyons in a hurting world. Maybe there's no such thing as a small act of giving. Every small gift of grace creates a love quake that has no logical end. It will go to the ends of the earth and change the world and then it will break through time and run on into eternity.

I would read later that those who perform five acts of giving over six weeks are happier than those who don't, that when you give, you get reduced stress hormone levels, lowered blood pressure, and increased endorphins, and that acts of kindness reduce anxiety and strengthen the immune system. Five random acts of kindness in a week can increase happiness for up to three months later.[8] "He gives by cartloads to those who give by bushels," writes Spurgeon,[9] and I'd think of that tin bucket with its 25,550 kernels of wheat. Maybe if all you have to give are handfuls, He might make a broken heart full?

But really—what if I were just trying to self-medicate anxiety? What if this were just a way for me to outrun the demons taunting me about my uselessness? Yet the happiness of givenness is a balm that works its healing even days and weeks later, and givenness does not define or prove our value, *but lets us feel the defining value of love*. Givenness changes our body because we become part of His Body. And we are even fed communion through our own brokenness. Maybe even in any of our misguided motives of givenness, even then, we are guided back to communion to reap the benefits of love.

A little girl stands there grinning with her lollipop, and I wink and grin back and I don't know if they call this the ministry of smiling or the ministry of presence, or falling in love with God in a thousand ordinary faces. But our Hope-girl leans into me, smiling at the sucker-licking girl, and whispers, "Don't you think giving is the greatest?" She's smiling like her heart might burst. "Look at her! I mean—giving is the most beautiful of all."

"*. . . and the one who gives a drink of water will receive water.*"[10]

There's this elixir in the veins, and giving is always the greatest, the most beautiful of all, because maybe giving is the shape of what love is—cruciform. Love gives. "Give away your life; you'll find life given back, but not merely given back—given back with bonus and blessing. Giving, not getting, is the way."[11]

And that's what I'm thinking right then, because that's all I know right now: Love must give to the beautiful people in the backstreets of wherever our feet land, beautiful people living near us and sitting across from us and streaming by us, and no matter what anyone's saying, everyone's just asking if they can be loved. Love gives and every smile says, *Yes, you are loved.* Love gives, and huge acts to try to make someone happy don't make anyone as hugely happy as simply doing small acts to make someone feel loved.

It's strange how that is: everybody wants to change the world, but nobody wants to do the small thing that makes just one person feel loved.

Giving is how we pass the holiest sacraments. It's the given bread and wine—*love*—that speaks to what heals the world's wounds. He who was the smallest, most fragile Gift broke into time to save the world. Why hadn't I come to it long before I had to blow out this many candles? *When I abandon self into givenness, the feelings of abandonment give way to abandoning myself to God and finding full communion.*

Koinonia *is always the miracle.*

You know how you may have words for something, but you

don't yet know the meaning of those words until you incarnate them? Some words only gain meaning when they have skin on. I knew those words to be truth. But I didn't yet understand what those words meant lived in my skin.

What's more, honestly, this birthday spent gift-blitzing the whole town seemed ridiculously small and insignificant. Beginnings always are, I suppose. First steps always seem like not enough, but they are the bravest and they start the journey to where you're meant to go. It takes great trust to believe in the smallness of beginnings.

"The Church exists for nothing else but to draw men into Christ—to make them little Christs," C. S. Lewis wrote.[12] What if being little Christs means doing the smallest, littlest things in Christ and letting only His great love make it great? Luther rejoins: "As our heavenly Father has in Christ freely come to our aid, we also ought freely to help our neighbor . . . and each one should become . . . a Christ to the other."[13] *Given.*

The broken world could change, the busted-hearted could change, even the broken could be Christ to the other—and He alone changes everything.

After I give a box of chocolates to the nurses up on the pediatric floor, I turn to the Farmer and say it slowly to him, "For an introvert feeling messy and broken and battling the edge of depression, it takes ridiculous stores of courage to keep reaching out, to break out of your comfort zone and give like this."

But look at what Christ did!

Maybe—maybe there's a Comforter who holds us gently in our brokenness . . . which is very different from a comfort zone that's a death trap to break us. And the art of really living may just involve figuring out that difference.

There is a time to be comforted . . . and a time to come and die into a greater kind of comfort. And like that song of given-ness running under and through the atoms of the universe, the Farmer says the verses quietly: "If you spend yourselves in behalf of the hungry and satisfy the needs of the oppressed . . ."[14]

And I turn in the shade of the old maples lining the hospital parking lot and join him: ". . . then your light will rise in the darkness, and your night will become like the noonday."

The light feels warm. Dappled on faces. The Farmer only nods to me. There's not much to say when you feel a holy change beginning: our broken night could become like the noonday. Light could rise in all this darkness—in us, in the ache of unspoken broken, in all this busted world. We will begin here and trust that this will lead us: spending yourself is how you pay attention to joy; spending yourself is how you *multiply joy*.

The angling sun sends shafts of light between the trees and onto us both standing there, and over his head, I can see how this myriad of insects had webbed their way in the beams, ascending and descending like glory bits from seraphs' wings. *I was made for this. The universe was made for giving. Givenness.*

"Every Christian," wrote Lewis, "is to become a little Christ. The whole purpose of becoming a Christian is simply nothing else . . . It is even doubtful, you know, whether the whole universe was created for any other purpose."[15]

We exist to be Little Christs. Not Little Ladder Climbers. Not Little Control Freaks. Not Little Convenience Dwellers. Simply little giving Christs. Not ever in a way that's divine, but simply, always, and in every way, disciples.

The term *Christian* means exactly that—"little Christ" . . . and that ending in the original Greek—*ianos*—it means to be patterned after something. The cross on my wrist—I am beginning to feel the pattern, the form, of everything. Dietrich

Bonhoeffer's words reverberate: "When Christ calls a man, He bids him come and die."[16] And Lewis leans in: "Christ says 'Give me All. I don't want so much of your time and so much of your money and so much of your work: I want you. I have not come to torment your natural self, but to kill it.'"[17]

Come die. In a thousand ways. "*Give Me all. I want you. I want you all.*" Give not only all my best, but even all my brokenness?

Standing there with the Farmer under the canopy of maples, I remembered Lewis's words echoing Christ: "I don't want to cut off a branch here and a branch there, I want to have the whole tree down . . . Hand over the whole natural self, all the desires which you think innocent as well as the ones you think wicked—the whole outfit. I will give you a new self instead. In fact, I will give you Myself: my own will shall become yours."[18]

It's like an echo of communion, of that intimate exchange of the givenness in my brokenness and the givenness of His acceptance. "All His is mine and all mine is His." *My own will shall become yours.* "Both harder and easier than what we are all trying to do."[19] It's like Lewis knows what I'm thinking.

You have noticed, I expect, that Christ Himself sometimes describes the Christian way as very hard, sometimes as very easy. He says, "Take up your Cross"—in other words, it is like going to be beaten to death in a concentration camp. Next minute He says, "My yoke is easy and my burden light." He means both . . .

The terrible thing, the almost impossible thing, is to hand over your whole self—all your wishes and precautions—to Christ. But it is far easier than what we are all trying to do instead. For what we are trying to do is to remain what we call "ourselves," to keep personal happiness as our great aim in life, and yet at the same time to be "good" . . . If I want to produce wheat, the change must go deeper than the surface. I must be ploughed up and re-sown.[20]

Hand over your whole self. Your whole broken self. *Givenness*. Because this is far easier than pretending to be whole and not broken.

There is a strange sense of surrender happening, a surrender in all things. The heart has to be broken and plowed and re-sown if it's going to yield. The change must go deeper than the surface. This is only the beginning. There's a bucket of wheat at the back door—time—and there's enough given to you to satisfy your soul—everything you need. And if you want your life to yield, there has to be a yielding in the soul. There is a plowing that breaks your soul to grow you.

I reach over and find Hope's hand.

"A good day, Mama, a good birthday day." She swings my hand high like those kids at the park. Her smile feels like grace.

"Nah." The Farmer grins, Shalom swinging from his arm. "A great day. The best day."

"The kids at the park, at the dollar store, the family in the diner," Shalom singsongs the day back to us, all our boys ahead of us walking back to the van. "That old man behind us at the coffee shop, those mamas with the babies in the strollers, the family at the grocery store we surprised by buying everything in their cart, and Mr. Bender at the nursing home and all his songs."

We lost the day in love. You can be glued to a screen or glued to your schedule or glued to your stuff—and maybe that's just a bit of lost living. You can be a slave to getting ahead, a slave to the clock, a slave to convenience, a slave to some ill-advised American dream—and maybe that's a lot of lost living. Maybe even in a bit of brokenness, grace moves in you to get up and give to people you love and people you're learning to love, to go to the park and laugh with your kids or any kids, to give an elderly woman a hand and a listening ear and the gift of presence—that's large living.

The greatest living always happens through the givenness.

When the whole crazy tribe of us GIFTers are nearly back to where we parked, Hope leans in, lays her head on my shoulder. We walk the last little bit like this, she and I. Wisps of her hair in the wind brush my cheek. The membrane between the sacred and the everyday breaks, and all is sacred in the givenness—the givenness of God through everything, the surrender of every-thing to Him. There is still light in the universe and wind in the world that moves in this given rhythm. There is still time to be given.

When what blows from the east sings through the wheat, it can sound like an answer to prayer. There's a way to break brokenness. And what if you let it fully come . . . let it come?

Six

What's Even Better than a Bucket List

Cruciform self-giving is the distinctive dimension of holiness.

MICHAEL GORMAN

I'd been dangerously anemic for weeks, feeling like I was a wet sheet of paper and the story was falling apart right in the middle, right where things were supposed to get exciting.

Out my bedroom window, the rain's coming straight down on the farm like an honest pouring. Another doctor's appointment in an hour to stick a needle into the bluing vein and draw out the lifeblood to see if there's enough iron in it. No surprise there, really. That my blood would lack the element required to produce steel. I keep praying like a fool that the cross on my wrist—its iron is seeping into me, its strength forming me. Any kind of love that lacks the iron of the cross in it is anemic love.

Keeping ink on the nightstand can be a kind of curative, my intravenous needle to remember the *eucharisteo* every night and send a bit of the thanks into the blood. And, now to ink a cross on my wrist every morning to re-member the *koinonia*, to draw cruciform communion from my believing head to my forgetting heart. This cross is a sign of my believing, that I am "called into the *koinonia* of His Son, Jesus Christ."[1] I know this. The *eucha- risteo* precedes the miracle, and the miracle is always, always *koinonia*. But maybe I haven't been living it long enough yet?

Wash my paling face at the bathroom mirror. The woman in the mirror is a wide-eyed deer caught in the headlights, life running her down, and she's desperate to know: *How can you believe there is enough in you of any value? How do you believe there is enough of you to live given—and be wanted?*

The wheat in the fields needed this rain that's sheeting down like some upstairs plumbing let loose. The sky slides down the windowpane next to the bathroom mirror like something a bit busted.

I need these questions, need answers to fall, to grow something in me strong enough to withstand this broken life. If I want to truly Give It Forward Today, if I want to be the gift, don't I have to believe there's enough in me that's a gift to give forward? Maybe we believe in Jesus; we just don't always believe in Him *working in us*.

The cold tap water feels good splashed on my face, running down my neck. It feels strange, even wrong to believe He could find any value in my tarnished brokenness. But didn't He, somehow? Didn't He believe it was worth redeeming, renewing, resurrecting, to make all into more than enough, in spite of my brokenness and through it? That cross on the wrist, wasn't it a sign of Jesus' believing? Isn't the cross a sign of Christ believing in us, believing that the busted are to be believed in? Which feels unbelievable.

The slowing rain seems like a bestowing, belief growing.

Lotion massaged slowly into dry and chapped palms. Rubbed into the broken creases across the backs of my hands. There was what an Orthodox Hasidic rabbi had said on a flight westward.

He'd put his prayer shawl in the overhead compartment and sat down, sweeping aside the tassels dangling from his pockets. And somewhere over the mountains, the light thick above the clouds, the rabbi had turned to me, mid-conversation. "Why do you people always say it's about having a strong belief in God? Who sits with the knowing that God's belief in you is even stronger than yours in Him?"

I'd put down my Styrofoam cup of black coffee and tried to read the rabbi's face. He'd leaned forward in his seat and tilted his head so he could look at me directly. "You may believe in God, but never forget—it's *God* who believes in *you*."

He looked out the window and pointed. "Every morning that the sun rises and you get to rise? That's God saying He believes in you, that He believes in the story He's writing through you. He believes in *you* as a gift the world *needs*."

God's mercies are new every morning—not as an obligation to you, but as an affirmation of you.

Was I living my life like I fully believed *that*?

I'd nodded slowly, and instinctively reached my thumb over, tracing the faint cross rubbed into my left wrist. *Christ is in me—so God can't help but believe in me!*

"A bruised reed he will not break, and a smoldering wick he will not snuff out."[2] God made the work of Jesus to "bind up the brokenhearted"[3] and there is more belovedness in Christ for us than there ever is brokenness in us. When Jesus is gracious to us, why would we be cruel to ourselves? "Weaknesses do not debar us from mercy; rather they incline God to us the more," seventeenth-century Anglican pastor Richard Sibbes wrote, echoing Psalm 78:39: "He remembered that they were but flesh, a passing breeze that does not return."[4]

I'm the broken . . . and I'm the beloved. Were there more

healing words to be heard in the universe? Was there a more soothing balm for all my brokenness?

The moment God stops believing in me, He'd have to stop believing He is enough. *How do we believe in Jesus in a way that Jesus believes in us?*

I'd sipped down steaming coffee above the clouds that morning, swallowing down a bit of the eternal. And now this morning, the clouds heavy and low and rent with rain, I'm drinking down only that: belief is a rare kind of communion. We in our brokenness believe in God—*and God believes in us through our brokenness.*

I put the lotion back on the bathroom ledge. The clouds behind me are low to the east, reflected in the mirror. The rain's a rhythm of steadying grace on the windowpanes and the wheat is drinking it down. Suddenly, my phone rings. Elle Jae calls every morning to check in after running her kids down gravel roads to school. I decide to confess.

"Well—just standing here struggling to believe there's enough in me to have anything to give. Trying to remember."

"Hey, listen to this," Elle Jae says through gulping down her breakfast. "Last night's conversation at small group was about exactly that." I hear water running on the line like she's pouring herself a drink. "When Jesus chose His disciples, He chose imperfect misfits. The broken ones were the ones He believed in, right?"

I run a comb slowly through my hair. "Right." The end of the eaves reflected in the mirror is this constant drip.

"So you know how when Peter got out of the boat he wanted to be like Jesus, to walk on water, but he saw the waves and he began to sink?" Elle Jae asks. "So listen: who did Peter not believe in?"

I turn toward the rain coming down, wondering.

Himself. I don't say it aloud, but it's immediate. I get it. Maybe Peter didn't doubt Jesus in that sinking moment, the Jesus standing on the waves right in front of him, the Jesus he believed in enough to cry out to save him . . .

"Maybe Peter really doubted that Jesus—believed *in him.*" And just like that, her wisdom washing over me, she tells me to go and have a marvelous day and hangs up.

I stand there, left with her stunning words thrumming something in me. I've been called out and helped up. *Can I believe in God, in Jesus, in a way that I know Jesus believes in me?* Maybe it isn't enough to believe in Jesus—maybe I have to believe that Jesus believes enough in me to choose me. If Christ has chosen me, can He *not* believe in me? *Can I believe Jesus believes in me?*

And what do I know about living as if He does believe in me? Nothing can possibly separate us from the love of God that is in Christ Jesus.[5] *And yet I doubt?* Wasn't that cross on my wrist Jesus' sign of believing in even me? Jesus calls us to the abundant life because He knows He can empower and fill us with His Spirit. And if He believes in us and what can be given through us, how can I not believe?

I turn to the window. Grab my purse. Raindrops walk down the glass unafraid. Jesus still walks on water. Jesus didn't just calm one storm—He can calm all our storms. Jesus sings grace in the wind, He pours mercy out like rain, He grows abundance up through the broken cracks of things like wheat, and a bruised reed He will not break, and a smoldering wick He will not snuff out. And He comes as a sign to us, a sign of the cross, a sign God's reaching for us, believing in us, in love, in redemption, in making all things new, in making us enough because *He is*. And He comes like light through rain coming down. "Come, follow Me—come, I believe in you—*because I've come to live in you.*"

Along the long back roads into town, the falling rain feels like the kindest anointing of belief.

At the doctor's office, waiting on a blood test, I pick up the magazine lying on the seat next to me, the pages falling open to some editor's column.

The fireplace at the end of the waiting room flickers like a smile. The woman in a Mennonite bonnet across from me, she hauls her restless toddler up onto her lap and away from the heat of the fireplace.

"We all have one." A bucket list. I'm reading this article, still rung by Elle Jae's pronouncement. According to the article's author, a bucket list is "a number of experiences or achievements that a person hopes to have or accomplish during their lifetime . . . Whether it is written down or tucked somewhere in the back of our minds just waiting for the right moment to transition over to ink on paper."[6]

I pause, mildly amused by the ridiculous coincidence. Here I am inking *eucharisteo* on paper, inking *koinonia* on my wrist, trying to let a cruciform spirit form in me, to get me to pay attention and be present and to make Christ present. And now a writer is recommending writing down the experiences you could check off to break you out of your boring life and into the abundant, exciting life. *Is this what enough looks like?*

I finger the corner of the glossy page. The restless toddler's given way to sleep, splayed and perfect in his mother's arms. The flame in the fireplace curls against the glass, the rain plunking on the roof like a visitation.

I look up from the magazine. There's an older woman hunched by the window with a permed and thinning crown of white. She's shaking a Bic pen in her exquisitely bony hands, trying to get a tiny river of ink to flow. All she needs is enough . . .

And there's this kid in a too-small, faded yellow T-shirt, dangling upside down from his chair at the end of the row of waiting chairs, hair cascading and his rounding belly button looks for all the world like the one begging you to push it for the answer to joy—and for this one strange, beautiful moment, I'm looking around a room of glorious strangers with hearing aids and walking sticks and plastic costume jewelry and bonnets and belly buttons, and all our lives are woven together, breathing and broken and bound to this wide world and each other.

I'm sitting there in a full waiting room and I want to find this editor/writer and tell him, "Look, the whole lot of us are done with waiting room theology. We are done waiting for some elusive future moment to say life is good enough. We are done waiting for some big enough house, some big enough step up, some big, exciting enough experience to finally think we've arrived at the abundance of being and living enough."

I could feel it, a bit like iron running in the veins: we are done waiting around to be enough, sitting outside of "real life." We are done with *waiting room living*. Real life is happening, and it's happening *right now*.

What if instead of waiting for good enough things to happen to us, we could be the good thing to happen to someone else who's waiting? What if we could cure our own waiting room addiction by making room in our life to be the good others are waiting for? What if instead of sitting in life's waiting room, waiting for a chance for something good enough to happen to check off a bucket list—*what if abundant living isn't about what you can expect from life, but what life can expect from you?*

What if the point of everything is simply this: change your life expectations to focus on what life expects from you—and your life changes?

Upside-Down-Kid, his tongue's hanging out now like he's panting for something. Lady-Waiting-for-Ink, her glasses on a chain, she's making these hopeful circles on the back of an envelope across her thin knee. Sleeping Toddler's cheeks are flushed, his mouth open and breathing a holy warmth, draped across his mama's strong gardening arms. I want to cup all their glorious faces.

This is what I know right then: the world is brokenhearted and full of suffering, and if you listen to what life needs instead of what you need from it, you could fill the brokenness with your own brokenhearted love—and this will in turn fill you. What if you were not afraid?

Lady-Waiting-for-Ink breaks into a pure light when I lean over and hand her the pen I've found in my bag.

Rain's collecting on the window like grace pouring straight down.

The article stubbornly waxes on. "Although I have had the great fortune to check several items off my bucket list, many still remain: explore Venice by gondola; heli-ski in the Canadian Rockies; climb the hills of Salzburg, Austria; kayak the boundary waters of Minnesota; explore the Colosseum in Rome. As you can see, the list is long and ambitious, and it continues to grow."

Ambitious? There's a tin bucket of wheat sitting at the back step that's pleading with me to die and to grow a hundredfold. If you spend your life striving trying to get more, is that the way you actually end up with less?

Who needs more when He's already made us enough?

Why grow the list of what I want to have instead of the list of what I can give? Why not let the heart grow big with a love large enough that it breaks your heart and gives bits of you away? Does "real life" only happen when you get to pick some balmy destination and a cheap flight itinerary? Or is "real life" when you choose to be bread to all kinds of hungry? And maybe this is how your soul truly gets fed anyway?

I've got to stand up, lean my head against the window, tickle that bare tummy kid, kneel and tell the lady her eyes catch light, and ask where her spirit comes from and what joy has it seen. How does being present to their presence tether and untether me all at the same time? Was that the running dare, not to fly somewhere else to find enough but to be like Elijah's ravens to bring people bread, to believe you could carry enough, carry Him, carry God? To be His givenness, just five minutes to Give It Forward Today, to *be the gift*—who doesn't have five minutes to become a gift? And what if doing that gave you the gift you'd been hungering for yourself?

I run my hand across the glossy magazine page, try to smooth the whole warped thing out. The underbelly of the sky's scraping low and dark across the horizon, across the tops of trees, torn open. The rain's driving hard now against the window.

"Where do you want to go?" the editor asks. And I've got this overwhelming desire to dig around for another pen and try to clear things up. Ultimately? Exhilaration isn't in experiences themselves, but in exalting Christ Himself, in expending everything for Christ.

EMPTY, POURED-OUT BUCKETS

ARE ACTUALLY

THE FULLEST BUCKETS.

"What do you want to see—and, most important, with whom? Then just do it! Figure out a way to make it happen, and twenty years from now, you will not be disappointed. As we have the opportunity to check items off the list, not only are we given fantastic stories to share, but we also gain memories that will last a lifetime."

Is that what the great point of an abundant life is, that we have stories to share? Bragging rights on the seeming abundant life? But it's like iron in the veins. Before you blink and your one life's a tendril of smoke, a memory, a vapor, gone, know this: you are where you are for such a time as this—*not to make an impression, but to make a difference*. We aren't here to one-up one another, but to help one another up.

You could go ahead and take up that editor and figure out how to make an exotic bucket list happen. And twenty years from now, you might wake with a few more wrinkled folds and that sick gut feeling that you bought a lie. Because more than a time or two, you'd grazed up against this truth: no change in circumstances can change your life like meaning and purpose can. No certain place can give you abundant life like a certain purpose can. Like purpose and meaning and connection can.

I had a philosophy professor who once said that Freud may have thought life was all about pleasure and Adler may have thought life was all about power, but there have been saints who've come through fire who can attest: life is about purpose and passion and meaning. At the core of our being, we need both meaning and belonging to believe we are enough to be part of what deeply matters. *He believes in me.* What if the deeply satisfying life was found in the givenness of *sacrifice*—to something of *significance*—through the *spirit*?

Rain's falling through the old maple trees lining the street.

Viktor Frankl, Auschwitz survivor and author of *Man's Search for Meaning*, says meaning comes when one does something that "points, and is directed to, something, or someone, other than oneself . . . by giving himself to a cause to serve or another person to love."[7] Maybe that's how you peel back everything that distracts and cheapens and derails a life—*transcend this life by giving yourself for someone else.*

Experiencing the whole world will not fill your bucket like experiencing *giving yourself*, and finding the meaning that will fill your soul.

The warming rains come delivering life, and common grace keeps falling regardless.

Every soul wants more than a powerful experience. It wants to experience a powerful connection. More than being in awe, what the soul seeks is intimacy with the Other. More than profoundly astonished, we want to be profoundly attached. Communion, *koinonia*, is the miracle. More than seeing and experiencing something beautiful, we want to be fully seen and experienced by Someone. More than intimately knowing wonders, we want to know the wonder of being intimately known.

I wonder if this is the language of rain falling over broken places. What if living the abundant life isn't about having better stories to share but about living a story that lets others live better? What if the goal isn't to experience more of the world but for more of the world to experience *more*?

The sky's drumming on the leaves all down the street.

Isn't this how God made the cosmos—with givenness at the center and generosity as this broken path to abundance? Look at us all in this waiting room. Look at us all wandering around a spinning planet with these bucket lists, desperate to fill ourselves up with meaning, *when meaning comes from emptying ourselves out.*

That Hasidic rabbi on that flight headed west, he'd picked up a full water bottle off my tray. "You know how we all want more?" He holds up the full-to-the-top water bottle in front of me. "Look at this. You can't have more unless you pour out. You can only receive more as you pour yourself out." And then he'd tipped the water bottle over my empty Styrofoam coffee cup, and I watched the water pour, and I felt upended and it felt about perfect. When you are filled to the brim with the enoughness of Christ, the only way you can possibly have more is to pour yourself out. The only way to more life is by pouring more of yourself out.

I'd looked over at the rabbi with my flickering smile. *God believes in me. Christ in me makes me enough. I have more and become more, the more I pour out.*

I look around the waiting room, the sky pouring out over all of us, raining down. The abundant life doesn't have a bucket list as much as it has an empty bucket—*the givenness of pouring out.*

That cross on my wrist where I used to self-harm, that cross keeps relentlessly suturing me together. And it might heal the world through this broken, vulnerable way:

> Have this same attitude in yourselves which was in Christ
> Jesus . . . who . . . emptied Himself [without renouncing or
> diminishing His deity, but only temporarily giving up the out-
> ward expression of divine equality and His rightful dignity]
> by assuming the form of a bond-servant . . . He humbled
> Himself [still further] by becoming obedient [to the Father]
> to the point of death, even death on a cross.[8]

This is profound mystery: *God became emptied of God.*

When God pulled on skin, when He rounded small in a womb and a billion cells broke and grew into God-the-flesh, He emptied Himself. His emptying, His *kenosis*, was a glorious self-renunciation. Jesus, wooed by the interests of others, "emptied Himself, taking the form of a bond-servant, and [was] made in the likeness of men." He emptied of His will and offered Himself to His Father's will alone because this alone is abundance. Jesus' self-emptying hid His divinity but became the window through which we saw divine majesty.

At the end of the waiting room, a mother cradles her swaddled one to herself and I can hear the swallowing, suckling, the givenness of a woman so a child lives.

We are most fully Christlike when we are most emptying. Most emptying like a cross. Cruciformity is the form of God. Conformity to *cruciformity* is how we take the form of Christlikeness.

The sky's rent wide open with sheeting rain, as if the world's code just got cracked open.

"They seem a bit behind in here today," the lady with my pen says, nods toward the nurses striding through the doors. "You here to see Dr. Reid too?" she asks in a raspy whisper.

"Just to get my blood tested." I return her smile, lean forward to lay the magazine on the table between us.

"Checkup." She slips the lid on the pen, the greying light in her eye as she looks up at me. "Cancer."

I nod, hoping my eyes speak the ache in my heart.

"You know what? Dr. Reid said the last time I was in here, that in our human bodies, the cells that only benefit themselves are known as cancer."

It's like the whole waiting room has gone dead quiet.

"I think about that a lot. 'The cells that only benefit themselves are known as cancer.'" She pats her bag. "Thanks again for the pen, dear."

I swallow and falter. I can't hear anything but the ringing of her words.

How had I never known that cancer is the cells that only take for themselves? *Cancer is what refuses to die to self.*

The waiting room's heavy with the scent of old perfume, with us dying and trying to live, and I wonder if that isn't a better way to live than carrying around a bucket to fill up: live for something worth dying for. Let love break into you and mess with you and loosen you up and make you laugh and cry and give and hurt because this is the only way to really live. Bucket list or not, don't waste a minute of your life on anything less. Don't waste a minute on anything less than what lasts for all eternity.

I'd once met a preacher man with a PhD who lost his mother when he was only two years old. He was one of five poor kids in Kansas, and she had grabbed her husband's hand and whispered her last words: "Always keep eternity before them."

No bucket list. Just five words. *Always keep eternity before them.* Think of eternity, and live backward from that. Maybe all that ever matters is to live backward from this guaranteed moment in your future:

> "Then the King will say to those on his right, 'Enter, you who are blessed by my Father! . . . I was hungry and you fed me, I was thirsty and you gave me a drink, I was homeless and you gave me a room, I was shivering and you gave me clothes, I was sick and you stopped to visit, I was in prison and you came to me' . . .
>
> "Then those 'goats' are going to say . . . 'When did we

ever see you hungry or thirsty or homeless or shivering or sick or in prison and didn't help?' He will answer them, 'I'm telling the solemn truth: Whenever you failed to do one of these things to someone who was being overlooked or ignored, that was me—you failed to do it to me.'"[9]

Looks like? Jesus won't be asking to see any bucket lists. Giving a glass of cold water in Jesus' name may be more fulfilling in the long run than filling your own bucket.

The belly-flashing kid's jumping on the brown-cushioned chair. The older lady, her red lipstick seeping into fine wrinkled lips, she's chuckling over the raucous. The gas fireplace blazes on and there's this strange new burning in my bones. More than any bucket list of merely exploring the world, you could live an empty bucket list of expending all for the world. *Where are the people ready to do hard and holy things?*

Had I realized it quite like this before? *When you fail to care for others, you don't care for yourself. When you help others live better, it's your life that gets better.*

That's what I feel in my bones—*faith is a glorious death experience.* Faith is a glorious death experience: death to the law, death to the flesh, death to the flash of the world.[10] Justification by faith is ultimately a daily co-crucifixion that's ultimately life-giving.[11] The cross drawn on my wrist, it's drawing me into something, into a holy experience my soul craves.

I'm called.

The nurse calls me. Lay out my arm there on the table. Penned cross there at the willing, surrendered wrist. The nurse draws blood. I can feel the drawing. All the living in this givenness.

It rains the whole way home, heaven poured out over parched wheat.

It's after dinner that I catch the replays on the news: footage of a tropical storm hitting hard in Haiti. Rain sheeting across a little, lithe Haitian boy running wide-eyed and terrified, desperate for refuge from a storm bearing down.

In the news clip, the shirtless kid grabs a bucket at the corner of a rusting tin shanty and runs with that empty bucket over his head. Carries that empty bucket like a roof.

And I stand up, stand up like I'm struck, a bell rung. And a note flashes up on my phone. A note from Elizabeth, my friend who is waging a flat-out war on cancer.

I'd given Elizabeth a red bucket of brownies the week before. I had given her brownies and a basket of food for a pasta feast—bread, cheese, sauces, pasta and spices, and grapes spilling the platter, because when you're killing yourself in a full-scale onslaught against stage 4 carcinoma with five kids at home, one with leg braces and a wheelchair and oxygen tanks and the youngest with Down syndrome, maybe someone needs to show up and give you dinner.

You know what I need to do? I need to send you a picture tomorrow with George and his bucket. I read Elizabeth's message slow. You know the brownies you gave us? They came in a red bucket. Which is now George's red bucket.

Why does it sometimes feel like everything in the universe is colliding in some kind of supernova of serendipity?

I've got to tell you, George absolutely loves how that bucket has a lid and a handle, and he carries everything he finds in it— and then dumps it out. George is five. It's her little George with Down syndrome who Elizabeth worries won't remember her.

I am thinking that over all—Elizabeth's words unfurl across the screen—the joy of the bucket and watching George carry it around, filled with whatever he finds, and then dumping it out? That's even better than the brownies. And you better believe all seven of us loved the brownies.

I nod, all of her words turning liquid and blurring. I'd given it forward, decided to #BeTheGift, and I can see Elizabeth smiling, her bald head gleaming, and George with his red bucket, like a celestial eruption in her darkness, gathering up just whatever he finds—and finding exactly that more than good enough. And then going around pouring that ordinary glory out. And all I can think, what everything in the universe seems to be saying, is what I text back to her: So it looks like— the bucket is more meaningful emptier than full.

That, she types back. That's the whole point. Who needs a bucket list? Empty, poured-out buckets are actually the fullest buckets.

Does she know how I've just sat in a waiting room and read this article that's burned me up more than a bit? Does she know my heart's slamming up against these thin walls and drowning in this strange painful joy?

She's not finished. You know what? I am not going to die until I have given away everything in my bucket. All the love, all the graces, all the secret happiness stories. Hear me? My bucket is going to be EMPTY.

The meaning of being is givenness. Ask Christ.

The phone buzzes with Elizabeth's last words that fall like a blessing with the given sky:

Rain down, rain down . . .

Seven

Love Is a Roof for All Our Brokenness

Our lifelong nostalgia, our longing to be reunited with something in the universe from which we now feel cut off ... is ... the truest index of our real situation.

C. S. LEWIS

When the Farmer comes in after eleven o'clock from the field, he carries it in on his grimy shirt, a few pounds of dirt. I wonder if he feels the whole gritty world on his shoulders.

He finds me in the rocking chair at the window in lamplight. There's a book in my lap. He has no words. Before I can find words of my own, before I can say anything, before I see it coming, the tired guy kneels down on the floor. He takes my bare feet in his hands and starts kneading in these slow circles all across my weariness.

Slow circles across the bottom of my foot, pressing away the day with his hand, pressing back what hurts with his earth-lined field hands. He looks up at me. Why do I want to pull back, pull away?

Why is it so hard to receive? Why is it so hard to believe you are believed in? Why can it be easier to pour out than to let yourself be loved? What in the busted world am I afraid of? He gently strokes my tired arches, long slow strokes, then deep, pressuring circles.

And I try to simply breathe. Letting yourself be loved is an act of terrifying vulnerability and surrender. Letting yourself be loved is its own kind of givenness. Letting yourself be loved gives you over to someone's mercy and leaves you trusting that they will keep loving you, that they will love you the way you want to be loved, that they won't break your given heart.

I don't know what to say. I want to distract him from loving me, want to ask him about wheat and moisture and straw, about the corn in the bin and weather forecasts and if there's more rain coming across the lakes.

He winks, hushes my rising angst with his gentle touch, his hands working out the ache across the soles. A day can utterly exhale under someone's touch. And to let yourself be loved means breaking down your walls of self-sufficiency and letting yourself need and opening your hands to receive. Letting yourself receive love means trusting you will be loved in your vulnerable need; it means believing you are worthy of being loved. Why can that be so heartbreakingly hard?

Isn't giving love sometimes—infinitely easier than receiving it? Does chronic soul amnesia make me keep forgetting that if He believes in me, I am enough, because He is? All I feel is I don't deserve love like this—and I don't. It's a gift, and in the pure givenness, there's pure communion. I yelled at a kid this morning. A son needed a ride into town, and I sighed too loud and said *not* today. I didn't read aloud tonight, and a little girl went to bed a bit shattered.

I know he can feel it, without need of words, my regrets knotted right deep into me.

Why are you afraid to be loved?

The Farmer's kneeling down in front of me with my filthy feet in his work-etched hands. There's a kind of mutual surrender necessary to communion, this decision made to receive the pouring out that I hadn't realized before. He cups my bare feet. Everywhere, there can be a willingness to be given. Everywhere, there can be the possibility of a vulnerable communion. Koinonia *is always, always the miracle.*

He looks like Jesus kneeling down in front of a woman caught in adultery, and it comes like a slow grace, how Jesus handled her critics: He deeply unsettled the comfortable and deeply comforted the unsettled. The woman grabbed by the Pharisees was given what I myself desperately need. Before all the pointing fingers, Jesus looked up at the wounded and rewrote her fate: "You're guilty, but not condemned. You're busted up, but believed in. You're broken, but beloved."

Whatever you're caught in, I make you free. Whatever you're accused of, I hand you pardon. Whatever you're judged of, I give you release. Whatever binds you, I have broken. All sin and shame and guilt and lack I have made into beauty and abundance.

Who gets over a love like this? In the midst of trials, Jesus guarantees the best trial outcome: you're guilty, but you get no condemnation. No condemnation for failing everyone, no condemnation for not doing everything, no condemnation for messing up every day. *Who gets over a release like this?*

You are Mine and I am yours, and all I have is yours and all you have is Mine. I marry you to the mystery of whole perfection, and I carry all your brokenness to divorce you from all despair.

I can feel it along my touched fractures like light getting in:

NO MATTER

WHAT THEY'RE SAYING,

EVERYONE'S ASKING,

"CAN YOU JUST LOVE ME?"

Jesus is not merely useful; *He's ultimately beautiful.* When I see Jesus as merely useful, it's tempting to want to make Him move my world. When I see He's beautiful, it's the heart that's moved, *and this begins to change my world.* When Jesus is only useful, He's a gadget or pill to make life better. But when Jesus is seen as truly beautiful, He's a joy that makes us *live better . . . love better.*

Jesus looks plainly beautiful in this man tonight.

And he's planting something in me: the grace of a love like this. A grace that will grow, as grace always does.

His hand covers my heel and he lifts my foot. Grace that covers your sins is always grace enough to grow you toward transformation. I reach out, touch his cheek. Grace given . . . grace surrendered to and received. It isn't a paltry thing, but the most powerful thing—the very power of God, a thing never to be underestimated. Grace doesn't ever *negate* transformation— but always *initiates* it.

The wondrous order of Christianity isn't "go and sin no more and Jesus won't condemn you." The order of Christ and Christianity is "neither do I condemn you—go and sin no more." This grace reorders everything in His radically gentle way. Just as God didn't give His commandments and then see if the people were worthy of freedom from captivity, Jesus frees us with His love and then captures our hearts with His new order. It's the experience of being daily touched by His willingness to save us first that moves us to be daily broken and given ourselves. It's His beautiful, relentless love that makes our lives relentlessly beautiful, not any striving to measure up or work to follow any commandments.

The Farmer's faithful hands work along the arch of feet and I can hardly breathe. It feels incomprehensible: God gives grace and acceptance *before* we break our sin.[1] Because it's His grace and acceptance that enable you to break sin. You never have to overcome your brokenness to claim God's love. *His love has already overcome your brokenness and claimed you.*

A slow understanding is unfurling somewhere between my lungs and rib cage. His declaration of "NO CONDEMNATION" is the seed of all transformation. Habits of self-condemnation can only change when they're taken to the cross of Jesus, not to the court of judgment. Go to the cross first and hear *no condemnation*; then go to the mirror and see deep transformation. There is always more grace in Christ than there is guilt in us.

The touch of my husband's hands on my feet is this tender loosening, a metaphor. There is a grace that's strong enough to cover the things I wish I hadn't done, and the good things I wish I had. The heaviest weight of condemnation can come for all those things undone.

His thumb massages around, around, across the ball of my foot. *If I could let him love me, I could let* Him *love me. I could receive His pouring out—even for me.*

I want to look him in the eye and say what I'm finding in this slow circuitous way: everyone is always asking only one thing—*will you love me?*

But I say nothing. And neither does he. We say what we're always saying without saying a word. We sit in the dark house, in a ring of light from one lamp. *Can those who feel unlovable bear to be loved?*

He looks up and smiles. I close my eyes, hardly bearing the tenderness.

But isn't this the way of love? Love *bears* all things?[2] "To bear," *stego* in the Greek. It literally means a thatch roof. Love is a roof.

Love bears all things like a roof bears the wind and the rain, like a roof that bears the burden of lashing storms, brutal heat. Like a bucket poured right out that could make a roof over your head to absorb storms, that gives itself as a container to carry the burdens of others.

Real love is a roof. Real love makes you into a shelter, real love makes you into a safe place. Real love makes you safe. *Stego.*

If I can learn to receive, can I become love that breaks itself open, that pours itself out and becomes a roof over another? *Stego.* No matter what they're saying, everyone's asking, "Can you just love me?"

I brave looking down at him. He's still looking up. *Let him pour out. Let yourself receive.* Do not be afraid of this kind of communion. *Stego*—come in and be safe.

He's cupping my heel, massaging slow, pressing it all back, making a safe shelter over me.

"You must be so tired." I hardly whisper it, not wanting to be more of a burden for him, wanting to draw my feet away but not wanting to withdraw from him. *Let the love come, be vulnerable enough to let the brokenhearted love come, and let it fill your brokenness.*

"No . . ." He smiles. "I'm not tired . . . not now."

The moment of givenness, of pouring out—of becoming a roof—it's like that.

Weightless.

Come night, he lies with his arms around this softening middle, his breath warming the nape of my neck. And the thought comes like a flash of soundless sheet lightning: anyone can lay down some money to buy flowers, cheap jewelry, a box of chocolates. But that's not love. Love isn't about how much money someone's willing to lay down for you, but about how much life they're willing to lay down for you. He lies long beside me in the dark. His hand rests across mine, the one with the black cross scrawled across the wrist.

After the tub drained tonight, I had seen these rings. Covenants are beautiful in grittiness. He'd left behind his sacrifice, the dirt he'd worked in the fields.

I'd reached for a rank towel to scrub off the scum. And I'd seen it on the inside of my wrist, the black cross I'd drawn on myself and remember those three words: Make Christ present. *Continuously do this in remembrance of Me. Remember Me— re-member the world, re-member yourself in breaking yourself and giving yourself away.*

It's strange how the remembering can happen when you don't expect it, how scouring off scum can feel like a sacrifice, an offering—a *presenting*.

The terrycloth moves in circles, around and around. I've been here before, and life goes in circles, and I'll polish it down to the pearl of great price. I'd wondered why in the world we have lives of to-do lists. Here's to tossing those sorry things, crumpling them, tossing and burning them. The dirt around the tub rubs away and leaves restored clarity: *To-do lists can become "to-love" lists.*

The ceramic feels ridiculously sacred, like a space to love him. Like all love languages are spoken in the dialect of time. Time to serve, time to touch, time to give.

I'd looked up at the clock. Time is for this. The hands on the clock never stop waving to get my attention, that time and my own hands are for nothing more than love—not schedules or agendas or to-do lists. Continuously make the ever-present Christ present. The hands of every clock never stop signing this: the best use of your hands is always love. The best way to say you love is always time. The best time to love is always now.

Practice brokenness and givenness and a bit of the kingdom is here now.

I'd washed out the tub slow, listening to what this all really is—the touch on the shoulder, the surprise note left in the unexpected, the phone call that comes regularly, the cup of something warm left without interruption. This art of being broken and given, of being the gift—I'd read that apparently it stimulates the longest of cranial nerves from brain stem to abdomen. These gifts of kindness can actually stimulate the vagus nerve that literally *warms up the heart.*

The gifts of love you give, they literally warm, *revive,* your heart.

What if . . . you never have to be afraid of needing, of speaking your unspoken brokenness, of feeling like a burden—real love is a roof.

Come in and be warmed by warmed hearts.

Light from the rising moon splashes across the wall, across a framed photo of our wedding day taken up in the barn because it'd rained that day. We had been in need of a roof. I've never stopped being in need.

The Farmer, he'd written out a check for the hydro, the vet, the phone, today in this Bic-blue inky scrawl. I saw him sign his name, hunt for a stamp. I didn't say anything, my arms full of wet laundry for the line, tired jeans, faithful plaids.

After the sun dried them out in the grove of ash trees, after I slung Grandma Nelly's wicker basket on my hip to go unclip their warmth from the line, I found him dangling on an aluminum ladder at the corner of the house, a tool belt around his middle, working on the eave at the edge of the roof.

"What are you up to now?" It's the way he wears his work, his dirt, like he's broken out of the earth, his jeans looking like he's wrangled for a piece of this sod.

He doesn't even look down from the ladder. I hear the smile in his words: "Loving you."

Two words, and he'd stopped my heart: *loving you*. Every to-do list can be a to-love list.

I stood there looking up at him on top of that ladder and suddenly I didn't simply want an empty bucket list as much as I want a to-love list for all this. *This* could be us. The wind could be in our hair like this, the sky wide with hope over us, the trials but stones on the way, and all the stones but steps higher up and deeper into God. We could be filled on the comfort food not of the world but the Word, enclosed in the broken-and-given of a vulnerable communion, and Love Himself would make us into love, pour us out, and make our hearts into a roof for others to absorb their beating storms. *Stego* . . . we could be a roof—a safe place. Ours could be a vocation of translation, every enemy made an esteemed guest, every face encountered made the face of Christ, all this, all this living, made into the cruciformity of Christ. We could be buckets poured out and crushed into bread to feed the busted and we could be dead to all ladders and never go higher, but only lower, to the lonely, the least, the longing, and the lost. That right there would be our love song.

He looks down the ladder at me, looks down from the edge of the roof. That four-day-old stubble of his carries a grin that speaks what you can only feel where the chambers of the heart meet. Yeah, there are those big-banner, social-media, camera-rolling moments with some imagined soundtrack building to a thundering crescendo, times when we think we'd all pour out our lives, throw ourselves out of a plane, in front of a train, show no restraint and brave the howl of the hurricane to rescue love, to save our love. But real love doesn't always look like that kind of heroism—that's more like Hollywood. Real love looks like a sacrificing savior. That's the holy truth. The real romantics know that stretch marks are beauty marks and that different shaped women fit into the different shapes of men's souls and that real romance is really *sacrifice*.

God is love. And because God is love, He gets to define love: "This is how we know what love is: Jesus Christ laid down his life for us. And we ought to lay down our lives for our brothers and sisters."[3]

Love is not always agreement with someone, but it is always sacrifice for someone.

Love only has logic, only has meaning, when it takes the form of the cross.

You do something great with your life when you do all the small things with His great love.

That black-inked cross, the one daily written on my wrist, it might cut into me like a tender surgery, break me and remake me, reform me cruciform. It all seemed embarrassingly small, how I ended up daily being the GIFT: complimenting an insecure kid, doing a messy chore, making a tired man's bed, taping a scrawled love note to a smudged and splattered mirror.

Why hadn't somebody showed up a long time ago in a

three-piece suit to tell me those small acts of intentional love actually trigger the brain's receptor networks for oxytocin, the soothing hormone of maternal bonding? That little acts of large love actually release dopamine, that hormone associated with positive emotions and a natural high? Why hadn't anyone told me: bend low in small acts of love, and you get literally "high"?

Real love dares you to the really dangerous: *die in the diminutive*. Be broken and given in the small, the moments so small no one may applaud at all. Pour out your life in laundry rooms and over toilets and tubs, and pour out life on the back streets, in the back of the room, back behind the big lights. Pour out your life in small moments—because it's only these moments that add up to the monumental. The only way to live a truly remarkable life is not to get everyone to notice you, but to leave noticeable marks of His love everywhere you go.

Love is so large that it has to live in the holiness of very small moments of sacrifice. Love demands you lie down and die in the small moments, the moments not scripted for screens, but written into the inner hem of a heart that can change how someone breathes.

In the night stillness of our bedroom, his breath is warm and close. His fingers find mine. Our hands lace in the black, the promise we keep making, even in near-sleep. *I will let myself be bent into a roof for you, a shelter for you. I will be your roof. I will be your* stego—*your safe place. I will love you.*

It's this. I lie there thinking how it is all of this. The real romantics are the boring ones—they let another heart bore a hole deep into theirs. The broken way is the beautiful, boring way, the way two lives touch and go deeper into time with each other, one act of sacrificial love after another. The best love could be a broken, boring love—letting your heart be bore into by another heart, one small act of love at a time—the way you touch the small of his back in the middle of the night when he can't find relief from the fever. The way he saves you a piece of strawberry pie. The way you hold your tongue quiet as a way of holding him. The way you slow and look right into the eyes of a child every time she speaks so they feel seen and known and safe. This is the love we all seek and love is simple and small and complicated and a kind of boring and the largest of all and love is all there is. It comes quiet. Real love is in the really small gestures—the way your hands, your feet, move to speak your heart.

He and I, we fall asleep at the end of a kind of boring day, heel upon arch, swaths of moonlight falling up there across our roof.

Eight

Why Love Is Worth Breaking Your Heart

To love at all is to be vulnerable. Love anything, and your heart will certainly be wrung and possibly be broken.

C. S. LEWIS

"I've got more than sixty years of evidence that every day looks better with bacon." My pork-raising dad's a streak of confidence on the other end of the phone. "And I'm telling you, even the end of the world would seem less like a crisis when you've got a good plate of bacon in front of you."

I'm flipping slices of bacon for breakfast. The only way to rise to the beauty of love is to rise and serve.

Dad's talking engines and pistons of forsaken old tractors he's found in junkyards and how he's rebuilding a century-old post and beam barn that he moved from a neighboring farm before the farmer let a wrecking ball bring the old testament down to the ground. The bacon sputters and splatters in sunlight.

He's telling me he is about to form up the whole span of tin roof, but I want to ask him what's pounding through my veins: What if you break open your one heart and risk pouring out your one life in givenness and you aren't received as being enough *to actually be loved back*? I figure Dad might know something about that.

I cradle the phone between shoulder and ear, keep nodding while stacking enamel plates at the edge of our barn-beamed table. Dovetailed together by the same carpenter who worked with my dad to build the house of my childhood, the same carpenter who built the gable I'd slept in all those years growing up, as the branches of the box elder scratched the roof through the nights of west winds. Three meals a day with all our grubby kids coming in from barn chores looking to be fed here. Barn beams for legs. Beams holding all of us up. Begging us all to somehow make room for Him, to make Christ present and become a roof, *stego*, a safe place for everyone who just needs to come in.

As the boys pound in, laughing loud through the kitchen, ball caps tipped backward, jostling each other about something, I mutter bye to Dad, who signs off like he always does, that he's got a million things to do and here he is talking to me and yeah he's got to go. Turn the stove off. Hope the bacon is cooked just the way the boys like it. How did the boys' backs come to stretch this tall, and how do I see them as babies I once held and yet as the almost men who hold a bit of me? And how do they see me now?

I should have just asked Dad exactly that: What if you take your one life and risk living given—and in the end you feel empty because no one saw you as worthy of being given love?

Who hasn't read that haunted grief in an old woman's eyes? Who wants to risk going down to the grave like this?

When our girls wander in with their eggs, the sunlight gets caught in their hair, slides down their shoulders, and they look like glory frozen in time. Shalom lets her clutch of eggs roll from her cupped shirt across the counter, and then turns and slips her arms around my waist at the stove. "Love you, Mama." She buries her head into me, her hair warm from the sun, and I enfold her into my own broken places.

What if you risk breaking open your own vulnerable need, risk exposing your own broken places needing to be touched by love—*and your brokenness is left exposed and unfulfilled*?

I serve plates of bacon around the beamed table, watch the straggling, ragamuffin tribe of them reach for their serving. And everything under this roof, all our brave givenness through brokenness, all our brave receiving, all our exposed neediness—all of it is a vulnerable communion. The abundant life *is* a vulnerable communion. This is what I want—but how do you build a life like that?

Shalom's freckles are awash in morning sun, and she's drinking down orange juice and the boys are arguing loud and heatedly over the periodic table. And Hope's looking out at morning coming across the fields, and I want to reach out and touch her—*we're all worth the risk of any brokenness.*

That canvas of the crucified Christ hangs up in the gable over the table. This vulnerable communion is a risk. Givenness is a risk. *The only way to abundant life is the broken way of risk.*

When Dad had called over this morning, he'd said his farming friend, Alan Bertrand, in his signature denim coveralls and a worn-through cap, was "just trying to figure out whether to spend the years he's got left restoring another one of those antique tractors he has out in the shop"—he'd sighed—"or if he should spend the time he's got left, the years he still had, trying to track down his daughter he hasn't seen or heard from in ten years."

I could see Dad in my mind in his suspender overalls. "And so, Alan decided?"

WHEN YOU SACRIFICE

FOR WHAT YOU LOVE,

YOU GAIN *MORE*

OF WHAT YOU LOVE.

"The tractor."

But—

You are whatever you love. You are, at your very essence, not what you think, but what you love. Open up God's love letter to us—He says we're all lovers compelled by our loves. We are all compelled not by what we believe is right, *but by what we love the most.* You are not driven by duties, you are not driven by doctrines; you are driven by what you ultimately desire—*and maybe you don't actually really love whatever you think you love?*

And the saddest of all may be when we give away our lives to insignificant things, things we didn't realize we subconsciously loved. Turns out—we give our lives to things we never would if we got honest and thought about them for one single moment. It's happening every moment—our unintentional, accidental lives betray our true loves and what we subconsciously believe.

The cross on my wrist is asking me, forming me cruciform, forming me into what I say I love. This is no small thing. Because nobody's ideals form them like their loves form them.

Why love the wrong things in the wrong ways? *Our ideals never compel like our loves.* The only way to the abundant life is to love the *right* things in the *right* ways.

I had shaken my head only slightly over the frying bacon, only slightly surprised, and the words choked out. "He intentionally considered the options, voiced them to you . . . and then decided *the tractor*?"

"Yeah. He already knew how to fix the tractor." Dad talked slowly, punctuating every word, like his life could prove it. "Little risk. But the daughter? He doesn't even know where she is. That was *all* risk. And you know . . ." His voice trailed off.

And I looked down at that little penned cross drawn on me,

drawing me, that's daring me to daily take the risk to be broken and given—yeah, Dad, I know, I know: our loves are formed by our daily habits. Our loves are formed by our daily liturgies. *We are made into what we make habits.*

"*Self*-sacrifice?" Ayn Rand, one of history's most controversial individualists, had questioned. "But it is precisely the self that cannot and must not be sacrificed."[1] Was that what Alan Bertrand was turning around in that geared mind of his? And what my dad was echoing? But how to fry up a pan of bacon and tell my dad: the self is ultimately never really sacrificed in giving, but our real self is ultimately found. In the sacrificial giving of ourselves, we give ourselves back our *real* selves, the self we were made to be—blessed to bless, given to givenness, loved to love.

Someone had once leaned over to me at church, nodded in the direction of our motley crew of a half-dozen kids, and then whispered to me, "What a sacrifice you've made." Like I had given something up. And I had shaken my head, this lump burning like a holy ember in my throat so I couldn't get out the words: Is it ever a sacrifice to give your love to whom you love more?

Sacrifice isn't so much about losing what you love, but giving your love on to whom you love more. When you sacrifice for what you love, you gain *more* of what you love.

Love is a risk—that's never a risk.

I didn't know how to tell Dad that, couldn't stop shaking my head. None of what he was saying made sense. *And yet it did. I knew how it did because I'd lived it.*

"Look." Dad had been unashamedly frank, right about when the bacon was crisping. "Do we give up what makes us really happy, whatever we are good at, a lifetime of happiness, to risk our lives on a relationship that might never make us happy? Do we sacrifice what makes us really happy day in and day out—for a relationship that has the potential to make us unhappy?"

Dad had this stinging point: you can sacrifice your time, career, sanity, joy for a child, a spouse, a friend, and they might end up forever walking out some door on you, spitting on your reputation, your investment, your efforts, shredding your heart and never looking back. And you can't get back the time and the lifeblood you gave away.

Dad had said it with this pain in his chest that I could feel in my own: *"There are no guarantees with people."*

And before I could think, the words had left my mouth. "Jesus said, 'Whoever loses their life for me will find it.'"[2]

Jesus risked Himself on me. *How can I not risk my life on you?* You may not love me back. You may humble me, humiliate me, reject me, shatter my heart, and drive the shards into my soul—but this is not the part that matters. What matters most is always the most vulnerable communion. Koinonia *is always, always the miracle.* What matters is that in the act of loving we become more like the givenness of Love Himself. What matters most is not if our love makes other people change, but that in loving, *we change.* What matters is that in the sacrificing to love someone, we become more like Someone. Regardless of anything or anyone else changing, the success of loving is in how we change because we kept on loving.

Who knew that sometimes if you don't risk anything—you're actually risking everything?

How to reach out and touch my father's broken places: love is always worth the risk because the *reward* of loving is in the *joy of loving* itself. *Love is a risk that's never a risk.* Loving is itself the greatest outcome because loving makes one more beautiful, more like brokenhearted Beauty Himself. The risk of a vulnerable communion always leaves you tasting the grace of Christ.

No matter what the outcome looks like, if your love has poured out, your life will be *success-full.*

That pain in my chest as my dad talked, his words aching with this unspoken broken, it all made me feel it: relationships are the realest reality—and the realest risk . . . *and the worthiest risk.* Because in sacrificing ourselves, we are guaranteed to discover the depths of our best and realest selves. Because when you self-sacrifice, you are guaranteed to find your better self. It's the longing for a comfortable safety that stands between you and everything you really long for.

Looking across that table at those kids scarfing down breakfast, looking into the faces of my own risk, like Alan Bertrand and Dad and the thousands who've come before, my own heart's pounding like a willing offering:

I am what I love and I will love you like Jesus, because of Jesus, through the strength of Jesus. I will love when I'm not loved back. I will love when I'm hurt and disappointed and betrayed and inconvenienced and rejected. I simply will love, no expectations, no conditions, no demands. *Love is not always agreement with someone, but it is always sacrifice for someone.*

And nothing will stop me from loving—not time, distance, disappointment, or death. Nothing will stop me from the risk of vulnerably loving because love like this is not a risk. Love defies logic and keeps on loving when it makes no sense because that is what love does.

Levi leans forward to catch my eye. "You've got more?"

And I smile. More. *There is always more.* We are living in His kingdom and His endless abundance of enough, of more than enough. If we'll but surrender to givenness. And I take his plate and give the boy more.

And I will fall in love and fail at love and fall in my love, but I will never stop the practicing, practicing, practicing, the givenness and the receiving. For what is faith, what is love, if it is not practiced? We in this vulnerable communion of broken-ness and givenness, will simply keep surrendering again to love because God is love and this is all that wins. Maybe it's only the veneer of things that makes this look like a warring world because, at its core, this is really a world begging to be wooed. We are all lovers compelled by love. Love or war, the answer is one and the same: *I surrender.*

Given.

Impossible things are healing here, healing us all under this roof. Giving away the heart—heals the heart.

The wooden barn beams hold up this table, hold up these planks where we break bread, like they once held up a roof.

Nine

The Miracle in Your Pocket
That Breaks Stress

You are to pay special attention to those who by accidents of time, or place, or circumstances, are brought into closer connection with you.

SAINT AUGUSTINE

A day is a pocket of possibility and it's always there, waiting for your willing hand.

I pin the laundered denims to the sagging clothesline by the flint lining of their pockets, oversized wooden clothespins holding them in the wind. It's blowing in from the east today, winding through the orchard, flapping the legs of all the farm-stained Wranglers like you can't keep a good man down.

There's something to loving the air and the country and the long gravel back roads, and the scent of sun-dried jeans and the grass and the dirt right under you, something to inhaling this whole given world and know this life is your story. Stress can steal just about everything but our stories—nothing can steal our stories, not even death.

Sling the wicker laundry basket up on the hip, head in to get lunch on the table. Our strained and knotted shoulders can feel wind beaten, trying to hold bits of our broken world together.

But I keep telling my chronic soul amnesia to surrender the idea of being the mortar that holds all our mortal lives together and simply let go, believing that the broken bits of a heart are sand in His wind to carve a better life.

When the Farmer walks in from the shop, smelling of tractor grease and honest work, the kids are arguing at each other downstairs like wild banshees, and I'm trying to corral my circus and my troupe of monkeys and there's nothing yet on the table to placate the man's growling stomach after a long, hard day. His jeans are grease-stained, his back pockets threadbare.

The potatoes are still bobbing in a boil on the stove. He's grinning as he reaches for the oven mitts. "Hey, guys. You all sound a little worked up down there."

I try to get the roast out of the oven before he does. He drains the potatoes. "Hey, why don't you all come on up here and help get dinner on the table." He's calling toward the stairs and the scrambling chaos of kids scuffling down there in the bowels under the house.

They crash up the stairs and Hope says, "I'm done, Dad, absolutely done with insane brothers. I have a geometry test tomorrow," she punctuates every word with angst, "and I have no time for this. Wait—the table's not even set?"

The Farmer smiles, sets the big steel pot on the edge of the counter. "Know what I heard on the radio today out there in the shop under the tractor?"

Hope frowns, skeptical.

"A study from Yale said the best way to deal with stress is to do a small act of generosity for someone else."[1]

I stop and turn, the roast midair, en route to platter. "So some study said you get the gift of less stress—when you bless?"

"Counterintuitive, huh?" The Farmer's serving heaps of potatoes on a ring of stoneware plates.

"You're making it up." I get the ham to the platter.

He shakes his head. "On the radio today." The underbelly of the sky scrapes the lightning rods on the roof of the barn. "Quoted some white coat at Yale and the gist of it was when we're stressed and we help others, we end up helping ourselves."

I cut the ham into thin slices, trying to cut through to the center of things. The juice pools in the plate, catching light. I'm feasting a bit on the confirmation: *you diffuse your own stress by diffusing someone else's.*

I turn in the kitchen and the Farmer's grinning, serving up plates while the herd of kids is laying out cutlery, getting cups, pouring water. I can tell by the way he's grinning like some cat that he's swallowed down meaning and he means to live it.

The best way to de-stress is to bless.

Slipping up behind Hope, both arms around her shoulders, I pull the girl in close, kiss her on the top of her head. "You? Looks like you could use a hug."

"Mummy." She turns, thinly half smiles, tilts her head into mine, and I rest my cheek on her hair.

I don't know how to love like I want. I don't know how to smooth out angst or stress or worry, but I know you either leave your worries with God . . . or your worries will make you leave God.

Honestly—I don't know how to be what she needs me to be, or what anyone needs me to be. I don't know how to become cruciform. But maybe life isn't overwhelming when we simply understand how to give, just in this moment. I don't know— maybe all there is to living, to loving, is to live into the givenness of the moment. She looks like she just needed arms to hold her.

"Attention is the rarest and purest form of generosity," is what Simone Weil said.[2]

"You're kind of scared about everything you've got ahead of you?" I say it into her hair quietly.

She nods, and I pull her closer, and she's so much like me and what if she ends up taking my ways of quiet desperation and I have no idea if I'm doing anything right and *what in the world am I so afraid of?* I can see the laundry on the line in the orchard, giving itself to the wind, pockets turned out and surrendered.

And I can feel Hope breathing slow, feel my stress ebb, feel it in the warmth between us. We all long for the belonging of communion and yet there's this fear of the closeness of the fellowship. Love is our deepest longing—and what we most deeply fear. Love breaks us vulnerably open—and then can break us with rejection. There's this craving for genuine communion—and yet this fear of losing genuine independence. Need can be a terrifying thing. I know—I've built my fair share of fortress walls. You can crave communion but fear being used or manipulated or smothered or burned. I have used a thousand buckets to douse any spark of a terrifying, vulnerable communion.

How can I keep forgetting? Write it up my arms: koinonia *is always, always the miracle.*

"We're here, and we're for you." I whisper it, press the words into a gentle kiss on her forehead, and maybe there's a bit of *koinonia* in the stress. Maybe the cross penned on my wrist is pressing the possibility of new ways of meaning and being and transforming right into the bone of things.

"There are very few men who realize what God would make of them if they abandoned themselves into His hands and let themselves be formed by His Grace," wrote Ignatius.[3]

YOU DIFFUSE

YOUR OWN STRESS

BY DIFFUSING

SOMEONE ELSE'S.

What would happen if the abandoned abandoned themselves into His heart and let themselves be formed by His cross?

I would look it up later, what the Farmer said, how researchers had asked seventy-seven adults to record three things each day for weeks—any and all stressful events experienced, any and all helpful acts, like opening a door for someone, helping a child with schoolwork, or loaning anything. And that was the full-stop epiphany of the research: "helping behaviors seemed to buffer the negative effects of stress."[4]

It was like finding your own pocket miracle. If your hand was willing, you could pull out a small miracle, a small gift—a note that made a soul stronger, a cup of something warm to soothe someone's knotted places, a hand to help someone up, open arms just to embrace the overwhelmed and whisper grace. Carry pocket miracles into the world, and you're guaranteed to find the miracle of less stress in your pocket.

I would read what the researcher said twice, three times, and once more: "People overall did one or two acts of kindness per day, but what was most important was when they did more than one or two per day, we saw a benefit to their well-being."[5]

There it was: **Give It Forward Today**—give numerous small gifts forward today, and you get the miraculous gift of less stress. Abandon yourself to the givenness of God, and you abandon a bit of the fears and the stress.

Busy is a choice. Stress is a choice. Giving yourself to joy is a choice. Choose well.

I would walk around with it for days: three gifts a day keeps stress away. These acts of kindness, they were like counting gifts, but even better. Small miracles in my pocket that I could pull out—and let abundance in. It was the most upside down thing—and it was shaking me up. I could feel the breaking in of the Upside-Down Kingdom: dare to be broken and given three times a day, and it breaks a bit of your own brokenness. *Bad brokenness is broken by good brokenness.*

Riffling and sorting through whole growing mountain ranges of laundry, I'd feel this shot in the arm, a cosmic grace, an epiphany about living: "For in self-giving, if anywhere, we touch a rhythm not only of all creation, but of all being," wrote C. S. Lewis.[6]

Maybe it is better to give than to receive because it's only when we give that we receive what we truly need. Letting that settle into me starts to reshape the broken places.

When the Farmer crawls into bed that night, he's chuckling. "I think I know what I want for my birthday—and what I'm giving everybody for theirs." He flicks off the light switch.

"Uh huh?" My feet find his under the sheets. "And that would be?"

"T-shirts." He's laughing. "T-shirts that read right across the front: 'Stressed? Go bless.'"

"Right." I turn toward him. "And the back will read: this message is approved by Jesus and the white lab coat life researchers at Yale."

"How did you know?" I can feel his smile in the dark. I love when he laughs there at my ear, and it's like you can hear the joy reverberating loud in his soul. We lay there in the quiet, the dog snoring.

"It does seem like a bit of a miracle, though, doesn't it?" He's still smiling.

Yes—a pocket miracle. The bread that we give to feed another's soul is what miraculously feeds ours.

Be the bread so broken and given that a hungry world yearns for more of the taste of such glory. Be bread so broken and given to a hungry world that your own hunger is filled in communion with God.

When the Farmer heads out the next morning, I watch how he slips his hand into the pocket of his Wranglers like a surrendered willingness.

Ten

How to Passionately Love When Your Heart's Breaking

Forgiveness is the giving, and so the receiving, of life.
GEORGE MACDONALD

Go ahead and ask your mother—ask any mother.

Love is a willingness to suffer.

So I'm more than a little mangled and frayed before I drive our limp rag doll girl into town to see the doctor. Our youngest has packed this fever for five days straight. I'm worried and worn a bit thin and why in the world does loving someone always make you feel so vulnerable? Love pries open your chest and pulls open the door of your heart so someone can walk right in and make this mess that remakes you into something more beautiful.

Shalom leans on me in the doctor's parking lot. And the moment I lock the van door behind us, I know exactly what I've done. I can see the keys' mocking little gleam right there on the seat, all saucy and smug. *Brilliant, Sherlock.* You've got a little girl with a fever of 103 and she's finding it hard to stand, and you've just locked the rather important keys in the vehicle. Mother of the Year Award right here.

And to top it all off? I haven't got my phone on me either.

Yeah, alrighty. Sick kid barnacled to my leg like an outgrowth, we get into the doctor's office and I call home, only to get Malakai. Shalom leans hard against me, her face burning like a torch.

I attempt to explain myself, watching the receptionist bite her lip. "Uh, so yeah—can you send one of your brothers with the spare set of keys?" My cheeks feel some heat of their own.

"Okaaaay." I can hear riffling on the other end of the line. "Okay, yep, got a set of the spare keys." I can hear their jangle teasing. "Will tell the big boys. Somebody will be there soon, Mama."

"Thank you. Love you. *And don't forget about us! We need* those keys to get home."

I barely get it out before the kid hangs up, and we're left at the mercy of a house of boys and a set of keys just a perfect seven minutes from town.

Shalom and I wait an hour and thirteen minutes to see the overworked doctor. And for every one of those minutes, I'm either glancing at the clock or glued to the window looking out over the parking lot.

C'mon, boys. Shalom sprawls across me with the limpness of an exploded water balloon.

By the time the doctor sees us, takes her temperature, swabs her throat, tells her not to wretch while he drills another swab down her gagging throat, pokes a flashlight into her ears, pats down her lymph nodes like a TSA agent, tells us to wait . . . and we wait . . . and comes back with this scrawled-out prescription, we've burned up, oh, another twenty-three minutes and I'm thinking I don't need to call home again, for sure, they'll be here by now.

When we drag out to the van, we're the last ones out of the

office, and the nurse closes the doors behind us. Locking them with her own set of keys and smiling thinly with her very own phone there on the desk behind her. And yeah, I'm just fool enough to believe one of the boys will be sitting there, swinging a set of keys from one blessed little finger.

No dice. The parking lot's empty.

I'm stranded with an inferno child, only seven minutes from home, and I called nearly an hour and forty-three minutes ago. And they know I'm at the doctor's office and not here getting my toenails painted pretty, for crying out loud.

And there it is—I'm the abandoned kid again, stranded for hours after school in the deepening cold, forgotten and pacing and waiting. The kid at the kitchen window looking out into the dark, waiting for headlights, for someone to come home. The kid abandoned for months at a time because of adults' debilitating mental health, left to deal with meals and laundry and a kid brother and sister alone. Is there anything quite as terrifying as being forgotten? Because no one is really dead when obituaries are read or headstones are bought or flowers are brought to the grave; death only happens when one is forgotten.

Okay, c'mon now. You've got a sick kid counting on you here. And you've got at least a couple older kids who can help you—kids deemed by the government old enough to drive, but obviously not possessing the functional cortexes to actually remember their mother.

Do they even have phone booths in this farm town anymore? Mental checklist: the one by the pharmacy is gone, the one by Mac's Milk, the one on Main across from the hardware store? Shalom's cheek feels like a little furnace against my arm as we drag by the bank, the dollar store. Her feet are dragging like lead by the time we reach the hardware store. I find a phone booth, drop in the quarter scrounged from the bottom of my bag, punch the number. Shalom crumples right down and lies on the sidewalk.

"Hello?"

"This. Is. Your. Mother." I choke it out, trying not to completely let out whatever pain's strangling up my throat.

"Oh, I told the boys to come for you—honest! Okay—one of them's coming right now. They just left. Hear the back door?"

I want to break, curl up beside Shalom on the sidewalk and bawl. What kind of parent have I been? Whose kids completely forget about them in their crisis and don't come rescue their own mama trying to help a sick child? I feel worse than abandoned—I feel like a failure. I haven't loved them enough to be loved back? It's selfishness that breeds selfishness, rejection that teaches one how to reject. Only the wounded wound. How have I failed to love them? How have I shattered their hearts?

C'mon, girl. It's teenagers and just a set of keys.

But my dramatic, overwrought, triggered self feels something far worse; *I feel abandoned.*

This happens: you become a parent and your internal dialogue becomes this sort of Jekyll-and-Hyde exchange. Parenting is logically complicated, theologically enlightening, and sometimes a bit psychologically destroying.

How in the name of all things good and right have I done so many things wrong? How do I hit rewind—rewind time and go back to being someone else, someone better, someone who can make them all be okay?

And my logical self tries to curl comfort around the angst of all my drama: life is less about a formula and more about faith; life is more than Good In = Good Out, but more like when

God's enough, there's grace enough. Life can't be about being good enough, but instead believing there is God enough—God enough for whatever our own humanity needs grace for. And there's always that: today's bread is enough bread, today's grace is enough grace, today's God is enough God. The question is, can I believe that when the suffering and the grief comes? And if I can—will it make me feel any less alone?

Shalom reaches up, pats my cheek. "One thing you can be thankful for, Mama?"

In a handful of words, the little girl hands her mama a sword: *fight back the dark with doxology.* I'm almost too wrung out to even grab it.

Eucharisteo. It can come like relief—doxology can detox the day. *Because this is how you begin to make the ever-present Christ present. And you cannot be love until you feel you are beloved.*

"You." I squeeze her hand. "That's what Mama's thankful for—you."

And though I don't know how today's story will end, I remember: faith thanks God in the middle of the story.

She pats my cheek like I'm some doll of hers. Some battered, shattered thing. Her hand is warm on these wounds and failures that can't even be uttered.

When one of the boys shows up with the keys, I take them from him slowly. I know I'm overreacting and triggered, but there's some hot lava building to let loose in my veins, my heart liquefying, and there's no stopping it, things blurring and spilling a bit.

Turn the keys slow and easy because you've been here and done that and you know this: love means holding your tongue when your heart is hard. *Or when it's breaking.*

MAYBE WHOLENESS

IS EMBRACING BROKENNESS

AS PART OF YOUR LIFE.

I wait, whisper it to myself, soothing, reassuring. "Love will always make you suffer. Love only asks, 'Who am I willing to suffer for?'" This is the severe grace of love making me real. Real love is patient and it bites its tongue. It lets its heart be broken like bread. I had never felt it quite so viscerally before: picking up your cross feels most like *patience*.

I'm standing there with keys in my hand. Love, before it is anything, to be love at all, it is first patient. And I'd experienced enough to know that patience is nothing but a willingness to suffer. Patience and the word *passion*, they both come from the exact same root word, *patior*, to suffer.

Passion has much less to do with elation and much more to do with patience. Passion embraces suffering because there's no other way to embrace love. Love isn't about feeling *good* about others; love is ultimately being willing to *suffer* for others. First coined precisely to describe Christ going to the cross, *passion* originally and solely meant the "willing suffering of Christ." Passion is what is fully expressed in that cross penned on my wrist. This one image is the exact picture He wants for a life. And His passion and His death are what He wants to share with us, give to us. *"Don't fight suffering! Join Me and embrace it!"*

There is no way to avoid pain. There is no way to avoid brokenness. There is absolutely no way but a broken way.

Isn't suffering the first thing Jesus promises us? Isn't this how we make Christ present? "I assure you: You will weep and wail . . . You will become sorrowful."[1]

The only way to avoid brokenness is to avoid love.

Our boy standing there in front of me looks like a man now to me. How I love him—and oh, *how do I love him?*

You are less willing to suffer for love until you know how His love made Him suffer for you. The essence of being

Christian is being about passion; the essence of being Christian is about being willing to suffer, to sacrifice, to serve, to live into givenness—for this is real love communion with God and people. *And with one kid.*

And if I miss that Christianity is about passionate, suffering love, I've missed its essence. For the love of Christ, you can dream about starting a soup kitchen or opening an orphanage or doing some world-igniting work that will usher in utopia. But someone, somewhere, sometime, is going to let you down. Someone's not going to show up like you need them to, someone's going to complain that you're not fair, that you can't do that, and somebody's going to make it clear that you've got it really wrong. There are Job's buddies in every crowd. There's suffering around every corner, lurking in every act of love.

And if you can't bear ingratitude from the world—you can't bear love out into the world.

I look over at my boy looking back at me. We both look away and then try to find each other's eyes again. And everything in me reverberates with that one thing I know again and again to be truest about love: *the moment you're most repelled by someone's heart is when you need to draw closer to that heart.*

I step toward our boy. If I touch him, will we both break and fall apart and maybe everything will start falling together?

Pick up your cross. It's the only way you or anyone else can know a resurrection. Carry your cross so this carrying of pain makes love. It is never the cross you carry, but your resistance to the cross, that makes it a burden. Absorb the pain with a greater love—touch a shoulder. Bite your tongue. Swallow your complaint. Still your wagging finger. Let yourself be worn down to love. Let your joints grow loose with love so your hands swing easy enough to give, to break and give your struggling-to-be-willing self away.

You become real when you make every situation, every suffering, every single moment, into a way to lead you into closer communion with Christ. *A broken way.*

I talk slowly, words coming like an offering, like some muddled clarity bubbling up. And even before I say the words, it happens again, like it does every time. When you beg forgiveness is exactly when you remember how you've refused someone else forgiveness.

"Sorry—sorry, I haven't loved you like you've needed, son."

Braving his eyes lets him see my fragility. My impossibly vulnerable fragility and how I've failed and been failed. And it doesn't matter if it's the constellation of my failures, or how I've been triggered, I simply know, and I'm swallowing, the sourness of this mess. Do I need to own this or does he need to? Maybe all that matters is that we're owned by Christ and Love owns us all. That cross on my wrist, it's pointing the broken way through. It's not just telling me what to do; it's ultimately confirming Who is in me. Don't we have to forgive because we are in union with Christ, who is in us, and isn't He a forgiver? Any forgiveness is only a shadow of God's. Anything less than forgiveness is like a Judas kiss on our own hand, a betrayal of ourselves and Christ within *by ourselves.*

I take my hand out of my pocket reach out to touch his shoulder. Lay my hand slowly, fully on him, like a benediction. Like a gift. *A simple pocket miracle.*

And I can feel it—Christ within. I can feel it a bit like a burning: no one gets to forgiveness unless something dies. There always has to be some kind of death for there to be any kind of forgiveness.

He and I stand in this vulnerable communion, a bit of the miracle to be had.

"No—I'm sorry, Mom."

I don't turn away from his eyes. *Do you actually only love someone when you love them more than you love yourself?* Do you actually only love someone if when they break your heart, you don't hate them?

Maybe wholeness is not reaching for perfection in your life; maybe wholeness is embracing brokenness as part of your life.

And I nod at the boy, the relief of a slow smile breaking . . . and giving grace away . . . his way.

How else do you passionately love when your heart is breaking?

The next morning, I tell my sister what an absolute gong show we are over here, what a mess this really is and we are, and my sister says it to me, and I try to memorize it, how it made me feel:

"You are a velveteen mother. This is making you more beautiful."

And I try to blink back what she messages, what's brimming—what's hard to believe:

"Trust Him in all this brokenness. *It is a gift.*"

Maybe—maybe all this fragility is somehow breaking the brokenhearted—into Real? Breaking us free?

What could happen if we all weren't afraid of passion—of suffering?

Eleven

Breaking into
Being Real

> *By believing against all odds and loving against all*
> *odds, that is how we are to let Jesus show in the*
> *world and to transform the world.*
> FREDERICK BUECHNER

I'd spent the afternoon with Mama at her place in town.

The truck keys jangle as we rattle down 86, headed back home toward the farm. I'd left Mama sorting through pictures strewn across her table like the past had come calling. Why is the past never how you thought you left it? That photo of my brother and me in our toddler bowl cuts and plaid pants, grinning over a tower of spice bottles looked like the mid-70s exploded psychedelic and plaid on everything, and I laugh right out loud.

I try to memorize the sound of the girls' voices in the backseat, the string of starlings on the telephone lines. I try to be present to grace. The photos seemed to make me feel it: the past is a memory sealed right into you, tomorrow is a mystery unknown to you, and today is God's momentary gift to you—which is why it's called the present. *Continuously make Christ present.* I've got a cross in this inky scrawl, right there on my wrist.

Hope remembers three miles out of town that she's forgotten her glasses on Mama's counter, so I turn around. The girl needs to see. And I didn't know then how doing that would ultimately help me see, but sometimes life itself can change when you turn around. It's grace that allows you to make U-turns, even if time doesn't always.

When I slink back into Mama's kitchen for the glasses, Mama's at the table, head in her hands, weeping.

"Mama?"

I touch her shoulder and she nods, looks away out the window. Sometimes the most painful thing is to turn your face into another face. A face can unveil too much of a soul's information. Too much, too fast.

"It's okay, Mama . . . it's okay." She crumbles into my arms. Sometimes you can hear it—the resonance between the drumming of your own pulse and the pulse of grace rising up to you from the darkest places.

"It's okay." I soothe, stroking her hair. There is no fear in letting tears come. Sadness is a gift to avoid the nothingness of numbness, and all hard places need water. Grief is a gift, and after a rain of tears, there is always more of you than before. Rain always brings growth.

An old card lies open on the table in front of her. It's my handwriting from grade school, this blotting inky scrawl, cramped and haunting from decades ago.

"I don't know how to tell you," it reads, and I'm trying to remember who this kid was, what she'd felt. "I don't want to hurt you, but I am sad and angry."

I wrote this? What in the world? I pick the card up.

"I am angry for all the times I felt abandoned. I am angry for all the times I felt failed."

I don't remember writing the words, but I remember feeling them. "I am sad I said even this because I don't want to let anyone see how bad it hurts. I don't want anyone to know how much it all hurts. I am sad for what is. I am even more sad for what isn't going to be now."

Oh, blazing Gehenna.

How did this end up here, now? How did she find it? And how can you up and break your mother's heart on a drowsy, humid Sunday afternoon with a note from thirty unsuspecting years earlier? How can a creased and smudgy piece of paper gore a mama right through for all she wasn't and can never change?

Mama reaches up to touch my hand resting on her wracked, hunched shoulder. She chokes it out. "You can't know how . . ." She bites her lip like a steadying, like a woman reaching for a hand. "How I'm far more sad for what won't ever be now."

She looks up, braves my face, everything fluid grief. "I'd do anything to get back there and do it all over again. If only . . ." She turns away again, squeezing my hand tight. Her fingers smudge the inked cross on my wrist.

Oh, Mama. That may be the saddest string of words that's ever been strung together: *"If only . . ."*

I can taste the words in my mouth. Who doesn't know *"if only . . ."*?

If only there was time for me to go back for do-overs of my own, say different things to the kids, only speaking words that make souls stronger, somehow live better, love realer. If only grief hadn't driven my mother a kind of hurting crazy into psych wards all through my childhood. If only my sister's skull hadn't been crushed like tender fruit by a delivery truck in front of all our helpless eyes. If only I hadn't kept a stuffed closet full of a thousand ugly sins. *If only . . .*

But there's no way back. Maybe life always tastes a bit like regret. Whatever you do or don't do, there is no way to never taste it. And though you may have to taste regret, you don't have to believe in it, you don't have to live in it, like rowing a boat that only goes backward, trying to find something that's been washed out to sea. It's God's sea. And that means all is grace.

Mama's cheeks are wet. I'm standing there like a fool looking into my own sadness over what can't now be—*because I haven't been all I could have been*. She's my mama, and I'm her daughter. And now I'm a mama, and we both have never stopped laboring, wondering if we will ever fully know deliverance into abundance.

There it is again: I remember how she once forgot me after piano lessons and I walked three hours home in the dark of a snowstorm blowing straight into my face.

And I remember how I was once the mama who left a child, thinking he went home with somebody else, who left a store and drove straight out of that town without him, and abandonment is always a soul's worst fear. We got the call that, before they closed down the store for the night, they found our boy fighting back tears amidst stacks of used Charlie Brown comic strips. Sickened, I was the mama who wanted to enfold our boy in a begging apology and the deepest comfort I know: *even when life abandons you, you are in the arms of God.*

I was the kid who called my mama a witch and made a plan to run away. And I've been the mama who's called my kids monsters and turned around as an adult and ran away for the day to my mama's. Mama and I, we're sitting here at her kitchen table, kids waiting out in the van for me to come with the forgotten glasses, and I can see the suffering right there in

Mama's eyes, what she's doing to herself. I know because I'd just been the busted and broken doing it myself. How do you beg people to love you when you least deserve it, because that's when you need it the most—and what if that's exactly what God does?

Mama doesn't have to say anything because her eyes are saying it all—she's listening to the lies that began in the beginning, that started in the Garden, that hissed with masked innocence, "Did God really say . . .?"[1] Lies that can look you right in the eyes and you can feel the hiss slithering right up the nape of your neck: "Just look at you—you're a mess, you're a failure, you're damaged goods. You aren't ever going to be good enough, smart enough, together enough, liked enough, wanted enough, do anything that counts enough, and your God isn't good enough to turn the bad of you around."

You can feel too broken to be.

There can be a lying snake curled between your neural membranes and his lies can run poison in your veins. Sometimes our deepest suffering is that voice in our head.

And maybe that's exactly the point—the enemy of your soul wants nothing more at the end of the day than to make you and all your offered years feel like so much wasted effort. He keeps hounding this relentless narrative in your head, this 24/7 pundit reporting live who won't stop mocking you: "Look around at your life—you've messed up, got it wrong. Look at all you've broken, all your broken—and you call yourself a Christian?"

Oh, Mama—you and me both.

How do you survive if you don't turn on the enemy of your soul and call him by what his ugly name really means: *prosecutor*? The very name *Satan* literally means "prosecutor." And his work isn't ultimately to tempt you, but to *try* you.

To try your past, to try your perseverance in believing you're worth anything, to try your patience with yourself and your whole bent-up world. Mama's twisting her one ring around, around—like she's trying to find a way out of herself.

He would steal our presence, our very knowledge of *the Healer's presence*, if he could. If you let Satan prosecute you, you will ultimately imprison yourself.

Make Him present—even where it feels too broken. It hurts to swallow.

This is always the weapon that the weary and worn-out can wield to silence the enemy's voice in our heads:

> Who shall separate us from the love of Christ? Shall trouble or hardship or persecution or famine or nakedness or danger or sword? . . . No, in all these things we are more than conquerors through him who loved us . . . Neither death nor life, neither angels nor demons, neither the present nor the future, nor any powers, neither height nor depth, nor anything else in all creation, will be able to separate us from the love of God that is in Christ Jesus our Lord.[2]

Because this is the thing: the prosecutor of your soul can't ever nail you. Time can't wreck your life. *You* can't wreck your life. Nothing in all this world can separate you from the love of Christ, and His love is your life. Your life is *unwreckable*. Because Christ's love is unstoppable.

What seems to be undoing you can ultimately remake you. *What if the deeper you know your own brokenness, the deeper you can experience your own belovedness?* I wonder if this is the refrain of the believing life: I fall because I am broken . . .

but I rise because I am beloved . . . and I fall again because I am broken . . . but I always rise because I am always beloved . . .?

"Mama?" Her cheek feels like wrinkled silk. "Please hear me. All that was intended to harm, God intended all of it for good. All that's been, no matter what was intended to harm you, God's arms have you."

Not one of us is ever too broken. "Give our Lord the benefit of believing that His hand is leading you, and accept the anxiety of feeling yourself in suspense and incomplete," assures Pierre Teilhard de Chardin.[3]

Without even thinking, my fingers find my wrist where I once cut, and the tips of me trace that cross, and even Joseph's suffering was the door into discovering more of God.[4] Suffering that does not break us away from more of this world and break us into more of God is wasted suffering.

Become that cross. Cruciform.

"Mama? You and me?" And words come out from some long-ago place. "All that's been is what makes us velveteen. All that's been is what makes you beautiful, makes you love, makes you real. Remember real, Mama?"

Mama looks up at me.

How many times had she read the story to me as a kid? *The Velveteen Rabbit.* It's what my sister had said was happening to us. What does it mean to live real, to love real, to be a real believer, to be a real *live-er*?

Mama murmurs it quiet. "What is real?"

"What is REAL?" asked the Rabbit one day . . .

"Real isn't how you are made," said the Skin Horse. "It's a thing that happens to you . . ."

"Does it hurt?" asked the Rabbit.

"Sometimes," said the Skin Horse, for he was always truthful. "When you are Real you don't mind being hurt."[5]

What is real? Real living, real believing, real faith? Real living doesn't always feel like living; it can feel like you're dying. It can feel like you are breaking apart and losing pieces of yourself—and you are. Because when you let yourself love, you let parts of you die. *Or you aren't really loving.* You must let your false self be broken, parts of you that you only thought were necessary. You must embrace your union with Christ, bravely surrender and trust that what's breaking and being lost is never the eternal, needed parts of you, but always the temporal, needless parts that were getting in the way of you becoming real.

Tracing those two intersecting penned lines on my wrist, it's like everything's being worn down to the essence of real: the cross.

"My velveteen mama." I touch her cheek. "The miracle of real happens when you let all your suffering create love. When you let the pain make passion. The passion makes you real, Mama." I'm talking to her, but I'm the aching, busted one preaching gospel to myself, trying to find the way myself. I'm reading her eyes. Holding her wrinkled cheek in my hand. "I want you to be okay."

Mama nods—closing her eyes a bit like a dam to hold it all back. "Want you to be okay too, girl."

"But you know what, Mama?" I kneel down in front of her. Look up to her, her hand gently patting mine, her lips pursed trying to stop the tears. "You're teaching me how to feel safe when I'm not okay, how to feel safe when I'm un-okay . . . how to feel how I'm beloved even when I'm broken."

LET YOURSELF LOVE.

LET PARTS OF YOU DIE.

OR YOU AREN'T REALLY LOVING.

The penned cross on my wrist is touching Mama's wet cheek.

"It's a needed thing, to be brave. But maybe there's a broken way of being safe enough to be real and un-okay. Maybe the bravest thing is to be real enough to say we're broken and unbrave—and trust we're still loved in our broken and unbrave."

One of Mama's white curls falls in front of her eyes. I tuck it gently behind her ear.

"Mama? You are the bravest when you speak your unbraveness. You are the safest when you are the realest. When you are the realest about your brokenness—that is when you can know you're most beloved."

I kiss Mama on the forehead and I can feel her press forward into me, into grace.

You are the most loved not when you're pretending to have it all together; you are actually the most loved when you feel broken and falling apart.

And maybe I'm just beginning to see?

I wipe the smudged cross off Mama's cheek.

There is a cross that makes us all safe. Jesus is drawn to the broken parts of us we would never want to draw attention to. Jesus is the most attracted to the busted and sees the broken as the most beautiful. And our God wants the most unwanted parts of us most. "Heart-shattered lives ready for love don't for a moment escape God's notice . . . The sacrifice pleasing to God is a broken spirit."[6] Nothing pleases God more than letting Him touch the places you think don't please Him. God is drawn to broken things—so He can draw the most beautiful things.

How can the broken believe?

"Anybody can shove their pain into a vault of numbness," I whisper it to Mama and the bustedness in both of us. "Anybody can pretend, masquerade in their cheap masks. But the brave feel their failures and abandon all efforts to lock out suffering. The brave let brokenness come."

You've got to go for broken. *Go for broke.* Something holy is happening in my broken places. *Let all this suffering become love.*

"Don't run from suffering; embrace it," Jesus beckons. "Follow me and I'll show you how. Self-help is no help at all. Self-sacrifice is the way, my way, to saving yourself, your true self. What good would it do to get everything you want and lose you, *the real you?*"[7]

I look up at Mama. *We're doing it. We are all doing it.* Picking up our crosses continuously. Making Christ present against the lies, right in the midst of brokenness . . . *Believe there is powerfulness in your brokenness.*

I stroke Mama's cheek, whisper it again like a lullaby, rocking us mother and child, rocking us two old mamas. "It's the brokenhearted passion that's like His that's making us real, Mama." Passion is a willingness to suffer for whom you love. Passion isn't about desire, but surrendered givenness. Passion isn't about what or whom you want most, but for what or whom you most willingly sacrifice. *Passion*—its broadest meaning is "to endure," "to undergo." That's the point, the sharp point: passion is literally about being willing "to undergo," to go under your cross and carry it for love.

Isn't that all there is? Carrying your cross is about carrying your pain in such a way that it makes it into love.

"Mama?" I lean in. "You didn't know how to make your little Aimee come back." She drops her head so I can't read her face. "You didn't know how to stop the voices that said you were a bad mother. You didn't know how to make your marriage survive. You didn't know how to let go of the lies. You didn't know how to go on—*but you didn't grow hard in the midst of it.*"

Blessed is the one who perseveres and does hard things. Tough times never last, but those who hang on tight to God always do. And the reality is—He's already hanging on tight to you.

"Mama? You bore the pain and didn't turn away. You were patient with the pain. You were passionate enough, willing enough to suffer, to let yourself be broken into velveteen real."

Sometimes it isn't your fault. Life breaks us. The fall breaks us. The brokenness inside of us breaks us. These failures and relapses and suffering and sacrifice and service, all our little-deaths, this is the painful grace that can make the willing velveteen real.

"Remember that time I called you from the airport?" She smiles in spite of herself, tries to brush me away with her hand. "Three hours before my flight, I'd dug through my bag, but it wasn't there—my passport. And you found it in my desk." The light looks worn down to golden across the table, across her silver hair. "You dropped everything, dropped all your plans for the day, and flung out in the middle of that blizzard."

She smiles, wipes her eyes.

"You drove those ridiculous two hours to the airport, detouring around how many closed roads and accidents?" Her laugh lilts a bit, and I love her even more.

"And you didn't even change out of your pajamas." I touch her hand. "You leaned out your snowy window, waving that passport like a victory flag. And you were the most beautiful velveteen Mama I'd ever seen. You re-membered me. That's the gift you gave me, Mama. You loved me more than you."

She runs her hand through my hair, and Mama, she can only mouth it: "Thank you."

Mama and I are ringed in this fragile *koinonia*, this broken giving and receiving.

"Mama? Your heart's beautiful—especially the broken edges where you let the love get in."

She leans forward, kisses my forehead like, healing grace.

Koinonia *is always, always the miracle.*

I carry home Hope's found glasses, finally seeing. Seeing how none of us may ever see naturally on our own.

But if we can be patient, let ourselves be helped, turned around, *loved real*—maybe we can see the way Home.

Twelve

Breaking Your Brokenness

The joy of the Lord happens inside the sorrow.
TIMOTHY KELLER

Standing on the porch a few weeks later, watching the daylight thicken and settle into a torch across the ripening wheat fields to the west, I wait for Joshua to finish packing up his car.

The car's sitting in the driveway, and he's ready to head away to university. He's got his keys in his pocket, the boy and I knowing about lost keys found and how to passionately love each other through our broken edges. He wants his hair cut one last time. I hold the shearers in my hand, that pair we'd found many moons ago on discount, worn now and oiled.

How to let go? I'd held the boy, cradled him in arms, in me. More than a decade and a half—seventeen years—I had learned and forgotten and tried to remember again—how to hold on and be his *stego*—his safe place—and let go. In our own story, he was the boy who carried my heart around under his arm and I was the stuffed rabbit, the one stuffed with questions and so many ideas of how things should be that all turned out to be a kind of wrong, the one still learning, slowest of all, how to be real.

He's learned my eyes and I've memorized his face through every seemingly impossible year, and I'm sort of desperate to logjam the gears of time with all my regrets, wrench a mess of years right back to his beginning and get to love him one more time, the way I always hoped and dreamed I would—if I'd been better and time had been kinder and all our hurting wounds had been fewer. Where in the world do you find a reset button when you're being pushed hard by regrets?

When he sits down on the stool for his last haircut before driving away from here for the last time as a boy, I'm a bit desperate to somehow turn the last time around to the first time again.

"Well?"

"Short, Mom," he says, sitting in the chair, and I can still see that scar on the side of his head where he fell when he was two. How is he so tall in this chair? "Just cut it short."

The years were short, son. The years can be too short, and all the ways you fell short, too long. The hair clippers slip up the bare nape of his neck. I cut slow . . . everything falling away.

Do I apologize one more time for all I got wrong? There is always enough time to ask for enough forgiveness and grace.

Then out of the blue, he says it under the hum of the clippers: "Just—thanks for everything, Mom. Couldn't have been a better mom. All the books you read to us. All the walks through the woods. And making me keep practicing piano. And saying sorry. Thanks for always saying sorry."

Trim along the nape of his neck. Fight back this burning ember in my throat. There is only so much time.

But I got so much wrong.

After seventeen years, there it is: I have been the broken mama who punished when I needed to pray. Who hollered at kids when I needed to help. Who lunged forward when I should have fallen back on Jesus. Until you see the depths of brokenness in you, you can't know the depths of Christ's love for you. Joshua's hair feels like water slipping through fingers.

There are dishes stacked on the counter like memories tonight, and there are kids sprawled across the front-porch swing trying to read the same book at the same time. And there's the wheat that's now sitting back in the jar in the windowsill. And there's me cutting our son's hair one last time before he drives away from here. And for crying out loud, there is only so much time to be broken and given and multiplied.

I never expected to get so much wrong. I never expected love like this. I never expected so much joy. *Be patient with God's patient work in you.*

"What does Gram always say?" He asks me quiet, his head bowed so his neck looks like an offering before the shearers. Yeah, if my mama's said it to me once, she's said it to me and the kids a thousand times. "It's not that you aren't going to get it wrong; it's what you do with it afterward."

It's not that your heart isn't going to break; it's how you let the brokenness be made into abundance afterward.

And afterward, I'd had to say sorry—no, I *got to* say sorry—so many times.

Isn't repentance a foundational thesis of life, of taking the broken way?

Martin Luther's first thesis of the ninety-five was "Our Lord and Master Jesus Christ, by saying: Repent, intended that the whole life of believers should be repentance."[1] If the whole life of believers should be repentance, then what is the call of the whole life of believers but a broken way? Reduce repentance to a single act at the beginning of your Christian life and you reduce your whole Christian life to an act. An act of pretending, a sham act of posturing, a feigning act of pretense.

One night, I'd taken that same pen I used to both write down the *eucharisteo* for endless gifts and the *koinonia* of that cross on my wrist, and I'd broke down, written page after page of repentance, of every sin I could think of that I had committed. What I had been tempted by, what I had done that no one had ever known. The day I whacked a kid hard and the thousand different ways I'd cheated me and God and us and them in countless ways, all the times I spit out toxic words and scorched hearts I'd claimed I loved but I had loved me more. Pages and pages stained with my bloody hands.

Repent. You are broken and you don't have to pretend you are not. What a relief. *Repent.* It's the very first word of Jesus' teaching—not love, not grace; the very first word of the gospel is repent.[2] You begin to break your brokenness when you break down with your brokenness—when you hand it over to the One broken for you.

If repentance isn't a daily part of your life, how is grace a daily part of your life?

Repentance is what keeps turning you around, around, sanding you down, re-forming you, remaking you—making you into real.

I cut away stray hairs over his ears.

Sorry. For all the Monopoly games I didn't play while there was still time. Sorry for not saying yes more at the right time and for saying no at the wrong times, and sorry for flying off the handle and for not flying more kites, sorry for not being more passionate, not being more willing to suffer for love of you. Outloving is the only medicine that healed anything.

THE CROSS ALONE

IS WHAT MAKES

IMPOSSIBLE THINGS

POSS*ABLE*.

There is still light. All across the wheat fields, there is still light.

Brokenness is always the beginning. Repentance, good brokenness, is the only way to progress in the Christian life because growth only happens through the seed broken open. You've never stood in the majesty of an oak that didn't come from a busted seed.

His shoulders broaden wide . . . so like a man's. The child had become a man. And that's what had been happening all these years to me, the velveteen mother becoming velveteened: when you commit to loving someone, you commit to losing some of you—you commit to dying.

Is this why the vulnerable communion can feel terrifying?

His hair keeps falling to the porch, falling all around my feet. Where people are living like Jesus, there will be blood on the floor. There will be a thousand little deaths.

What I'd give to have known: accept the tension of feeling yourself led to the edge of yourself. In the raw experience of "I cannot do this," you experience how He remakes you into someone who can. And our broken hearts are called to that impossible, because that is who He, He who is in us, makes us: the imposs*ables*.

Love is really love—when we are loving the unlovable. Forgiveness is really forgiveness—when we are forgiving the unforgivable. Repentance is really repentance—when we let our wrong loves be broken by the rightness of His unbreakable love. Faith is really faith—when we believe God for the unbelievable. Because with our God, nothing is impossible and our God is *able*, and with our God in us, all our broken efforts become poss*able* and we are the imposs*ables* doing the newly poss*able*.

Locks of his hair on his shoulders, down his back, fall away like years. He looks like someone else. Remade. Or maybe that's just me. The both of us—imposs*able.*

When I turn the clippers in my hand, there's that cross penned on my wrist. The cross alone is what makes impossible things poss*able.* And the cross alone is the good brokenness that can break bad brokenness and make you real.

Without your wounds, where is your strength? There's been childbearing; there's been being like a roof, load-bearing, love-bearing, all this cross-bearing.

"Cross-bearing is the long lesson of our mortal life," wrote J. I. Packer. "It is a part of God's salvation, called sanctification. It is a lesson set before us every moment of every day."

"If life were an art lesson," Packer continues, "we could describe it as a process of finding how to turn this mud into that porcelain, this discord into that sonata, this ugly stone block into that statue, this tangle of threads into that tapestry. In fact, however, the stakes are higher than in any art lesson. It is in the school of sainthood that we find ourselves enrolled and the artifact that is being made is ourselves."[3]

His neck is shaven bare now. He stands up. Brushes the shorn hair off his shoulders. And there he is at the end of boy and becomes man while we both were just turning around. And that is all this has ever been, a passionate process of turning all that's been into velveteen. God's enrolled us in this school of sainthood and the art that is being made is our real selves. The suffering voluntarily accepted, made poss*able,* is being made into glory.

Human-making is ultimately a function of passionate cross-bearing. Only cross-bearing will make you passionately human. Real. This dare to write a cross on my wrist every day and let Him rewrite me and all my stories—this was the dare to become nothing less than really, fully human.

"If you don't bother sweeping the hair away here on the porch," he says as he brushes more off his chest, "the birds will carry it off for nests."

I nod and stand at the edge of the porch and watch him leave, watch him drive out the lane and away.

It definitely gets harder before it gets easier. But it will definitely get better—if you don't give up when it's hardest. "So let's not allow ourselves to get fatigued doing good. At the right time we will harvest a crop if we don't give up, or quit."[4]

That's the gift he and I are giving and receiving, a real communion of relationship. Relationships only get to exist as long as they keep breathing in the air of mutual forgiveness, and he and I have found an uncommon grace. Grace can strike when you are in great pain and light you with the greatest hope.

I leave the broom there at the door. Leave all the locks and passionate pieces of us, left behind for whatever might possibly come.

Thirteen

The Inconvenient Truth
No One Tells You

*If today were your last, would you do what you're
doing? Or would you love more, give more,
forgive more? Then do so! Forgive and give as if
it were your last opportunity. Love like there's no
tomorrow, and if tomorrow comes, love again.*

MAX LUCADO

Would she know that we all came to her funeral, that we all
gathered when she died?

Our Elizabeth. *My* Elizabeth.

When our times intersect, when our lives cross, do we always
know somewhere deep within us, this is a holy thing? The cross
hangs there at the front of the church. The afternoon's caught,
thick and saturated, up in the stained-glass windows. Spring
unwinds in the trees outside.

Elizabeth with her George and the red bucket that was
more meaningful empty than full, Elizabeth had died, poured
right out.

I stand by her draped coffin. The sanctuary is heavy with
the scent of lilies and old perfume and the wicks of drows-
ing candles. Elizabeth, trapped in that dark, hinged box. My

Elizabeth had begun like every one of us—a single, almost invisible cell. Molecules knit together, mitochondria sending out missives, and we begin as a microscopic swirl. And then, right from the very beginning, we break.

Break, divide, and multiply, because what other way is there to grow? No other way to transform and begin to belong, this breaking and dividing to grow a heart—a heart that began in breaking, that was made to break. The heart beats and then forty weeks later, six trillion cells crush through a birth canal in that primal howl. Then in forty short years, everything can stop dead forever.

How can there be no way for me now to transfer all that I feel, all this grieving love still trapped in my chest, somehow move it to hers so she can know and carry it with her? Maybe she knows it now better than ever, but how can there be this hole now in the world, where she once was, and we're all just expected to go on? In front of me, a woman creaks the prayer bench under her pew back and forth, back and forth.

How can I tell Elizabeth I'm not ready for our conversation to be abruptly interrupted, that there's more I'd meant to say, that I'm desperate to say, and this chasm between time and eternity that's fallen between us is driving me a bit mad with grief?

Someone said she would rise again in the sun, rise in our prayers, but I don't know about that. When the sunrise pokes a pinhole through the horizon tomorrow morning, will all our pain somehow leak through it? Why is it that only once you face life without the loveliness of those you love, you can finally see how much you love? Why is the clearest way to love your life only to imagine losing parts of it?

A woman's heels clap across the back of the church. Then the near-silence of all our heartbeats.

I had another friend who'd stood at heaven's door who'd said, "It won't be any time before we are reunited, but for the mortal it feels impossible to understand the close distance of eternity."[1] Nothing feels close standing there by Elizabeth's casket. Everything feels broken and impossibly distant.

All I can hear in the deafening, unscalable silence between Elizabeth and me is this echo from the *Book of Common Prayer*: "From all oppression, conspiracy, and rebellion; from violence, battle, and murder; and from dying suddenly and unprepared, good Lord, deliver us."[2]

And yet don't we long for some sudden and unexpected death that keeps us from knowing we're actually dying—that keeps us from preparing? Once people feared a sudden, unprepared death because they feared meeting God suddenly and unprepared. Maybe now we only fear death because we don't fear God.

Someone across the aisle blows her nose.

Elizabeth's leaving, it was like sudden whiplash. I am not prepared. But I'd paused what's pressing, cork the torrent of everyday that keeps coming, pause all the living because she isn't living anymore, and I come one last time to her, where now there is only this void, this gash that won't let me through to her.

When the funeral director closes the back doors of the sanctuary, the bottom edges scrape across the floor. I've twisted the tissue in my hand till it's this whorled shell and my inner ears reverberate with a kind of crashing.

This is all I can do now to try to keep loving her: I can show up. Elizabeth would have loved that. Would she have loved it if I had showed up more? Showed up with the gift of an old frayed blanket and told her—not asked her, but told her—that we were going to the park with a stack of old books to watch the clouds? If I had called her back that time I thought it was too late? If I hadn't walked by that scarf that was screaming her name and surprised her with it as a just-because gift?

If I'd stolen five minutes, grabbed a postcard, and scrawled out three lines—"There isn't a laugh in the world like yours. You handed me a life supply of courage because you loved me like this. And yeah, you pretty much beat me at everything, but I win at this: I love you more." Why hadn't I been that gift more often? The ministry of presence is a gift with an expiry date. Everything proves it now: this is unexpected happiness, to be broken and given to bless.

The priest steps into the carved pulpit, his robes whispering. His voice is unhurried, like old wine, full-bodied and settled. He says last he sat with Elizabeth, she'd murmured, "I give this all up to You." The words echo through the vaulting space. How does it change everything to read suffering as Christ's invitation to follow Him to the cross and share His cross? "Christ goes to the cross, and we are invited to follow to the same cross. Not because it is the cross, but because it is His," writes Peter Kreeft.[3]

I can see Elizabeth's twelve-year-old in the pew up front. He turns and stares at her coffin, his hair hanging over his eyes. I had shown up when Elizabeth was between rounds of chemo. We spent an afternoon with the sun on our backs in a big window at that coffee shop on the corner. She had shown me how to knit the sleeves for a sweater. Her bald head was like a pearl.

We had dinner once with her uncle Joe and her mom and dad in that Italian restaurant up in Michigan, and her dad asked the waiter to turn off the music because we were the only ones there. And those million emails, ten million messages, and a handful of girls' weekends where we made the time for each other, gave each other the gift of each other, and all laughed like hyenas over steaming Chinese takeout and cried late at night over kids and motherhood and what it means to never stop this laboring and delivering. And Elizabeth, always the GIFTer, finished knitting those matching socks for all four of us. We didn't know how we'd ever walk away from each other.

She died on Maundy Thursday, the Thursday He mandated for us to love one another, the Thursday of communion. Koinonia *is always, always the miracle.* I can hear her voice on the other end of the line and how she would say it always unashamed: *"I love you."* Why do we not say what we mean until it's too late for it to mean anything? I can close my eyes and hear her laugh. Quick—open your eyes and see everything you can, memorize everything you can, before you can never open your eyes again.

Celestial blue. The ceiling over all of us and Elizabeth's casket is sky blue. Buttery yellow, the walls of the nave are this buttery yellow—like buttercups, like a warming spring sun . . . like the way she'd laughed. The yellow pollen stuck in the layers of lilies looks like lost particles of the sun caught in their trumpeting throats.

Elizabeth never once stopped battling brave. Not when the oozing cold sores barnacled the walls of her mouth and made swallowing feel like choking on razors. Not when the cancer made powder of her crumbling vertebrae and the agony of her collapse was titanic. Not when she started to leak blood like a slow death drip. Be brave and do not pray for the hard thing to go away, but pray for a bravery that's bigger than the hard thing.

Elizabeth tells me once, tells me a dozen times, especially

in the middle of the wracking nights: the longer she suffers, the longer she gets to love. This is always true, everywhere. Elizabeth didn't avoid suffering, because she didn't want to avoid loving.

Because Elizabeth knew "love is the most characteristic and comprehensive act of the human being. We are most ourselves when we love; we are most the People of God when we love,"[4] and loving like Jesus loves, embodying our union with Christ and our *koinonia* with the body of Christ—is the singular life work of the Jesus follower. *This is always worth the suffering.* There is a river over which every soul must pass to reach the kingdom of heaven and the name of that river is suffering—and the way to cross that river is a cross nailed together with love.

I stand by her casket, feeling what she knew: grief is the guaranteed price we always pay for love.

Elizabeth's husband opens his mouth slowly for the bread. He swallows down communion beside the white-draped casket of his wife.

The way through brokenness is, and always has been, to break the sufferer free from the aloneness of the suffering by choosing to participate in the suffering with them—*koinonia*—choosing to stand with the suffering, stay with the suffering, and let it all be shaped into meaning that *transcends* the suffering.

Elizabeth had asked me to sit with her through the cold of the chemo. She had tried to knit socks through the drip—more prayer socks, praying through every loop. She had chosen it: Be a prayer warrior. Not a panicked worrier.

I look up and down the pews. Rainbows of socks. People have worn the socks that Elizabeth knitted for them—Elizabeth's prayer socks, her prayers knit into every single one of the 19,800 stitches in a pair of socks. The pews are filled with them,

TO BE

THE RE-MEMBERING PEOPLE—

THIS IS THE WORK OF LIFE

IN A BROKENHEARTED WORLD.

a kaleidoscope of teals and purples, misty blues and greys and a riot of cerulean—shod in scuffed-up Mary Janes and patented ballet flats, sneakers, and polished black loafers. We are all shod in the gospel, in bits of Elizabeth, broken and given and knit together, and I could break down right here.

A violin plays. A cello. Wine, the cup of His suffering, it stings hot and dangerous down my willing throat. That's what Elizabeth did. She became wine, dangerous to my protective, barrier walls. You can't know the wine you will be during the days you are breaking and being crushed like grapes.

Are the most painful chapters of our lives always the most meaningful?

Knees creak. *Be Thou my vision, O Lord of my heart*. The notes rise to the blue ceiling. Elizabeth's father laces his fingers through her mother's.

All who love will ultimately suffer. If we hadn't loved her, if we hadn't let her love us, our lungs wouldn't burn with this ache. God knew when He beckoned "you shall love your neighbor" that in keeping the commandment to love, we would also keep suffering. And still He gave the command.

Love runs through us through veins of suffering. I turn over my wrist to see that cross there again. *This is the way. There is no other.*

Sometimes it's so clear: we can only love in this world if we're willing to suffer with the world. "God so suffered for the world that he gave up his only Son to suffering," wrote Nicholas Wolterstorff.[5] Suffering is at the burning core of everything because *love is*. We need not feel alone in suffering because God is a suffering God who pulls close at our call.

We can receive it if we want—*there is always more God*. In tears is intimacy. God understands because He stands with us.

Hundreds of us stand shoulder to shoulder in our holy socks in the church sanctuary, giving everything in our lungs. *Thou in me dwelling, and I with Thee one.* There is always union with Christ that we only need wake to and *koinonia* always is the miracle. I try to memorize everything—the colors, the faces, all the eyes. *Heart of my own heart, whatever befall . . .*

I had read it and never forgotten: the word *suffer* comes from the Latin "to bear under." Suffering is an act of surrender, to bear under that which is not under our control. I want to ask Elizabeth: *Is this why we avoid suffering at all costs? Is this why we desperately try to avoid pain, because suffering is a surrender to the uncontrollable?*

Suffering asks us to bear under that which is ultimately not under our control, which proves to us we have no control. And maybe that's too much for us in our autonomous, do-it-yourself culture to bear. Maybe more than we can't stand physical suffering, we can't stand not feeling in control.

I find myself slowly opening my hand right there in the pew. Isn't openness a willingness to be given?

Suffering quietly begs us to surrender so we'll win a greater wisdom, a deeper strength, a closer intimacy. Suffering says we cannot bear under this cross alone—we can only bear it if we can bear depending on others, bear the vulnerability and intimacy of *koinonia*. If we can bear depending on Him.

Elizabeth's casket looks small sitting there under the spread-out wooden cross on the eastern wall. The beam, an axis that could open a hole in the universe and let eternity in. We bow our heads. Intonations of prayer.

Elizabeth had chosen to bear under that which was beyond her control because she knew that under her were the everlasting arms of One in control. One who would never let her go.

Elizabeth chose to bear under the suffering because she humbly chose to bear depending on others . . . depending on us being a community, a body, human beings who belong to each other and who will carry each other, carried by the crossbeam of the cosmos—*koinonia*.

If suffering is to bear under for each other, then wasn't that always the call? In a broken world, isn't the call always to *koinonia*, to communion with community that bears our burdens with us? Wasn't suffering then actually a call for us to be a community, to stand together and bear under, trusting that arms of love are always under us?

Had I failed her? For all my grasping justifications, had I failed living *koinonia* with her and entering into her sufferings, participating in them and in the abundance of Christ? Isn't that, after all, why we're one body? "Contribute to the needs of the saints," the apostle Paul wrote.[6] Peel open the glued eyes and see the needs as your very own because we are the same body. "Do this in remembrance of me."[7] To make Christ present, to re-member our brokenness, we must take the crushed and broken bread and swallow down our communion with a broken community.

Candlelight chases rising smoke. Elizabeth's life lies completed, but I am unraveling it: *entering each other's suffering is how to make life communion.* Any shattered heart becomes my shattered heart. There is no apathy in the body of Christ: apathy is what amputates members and limbs of the body. There is no distance in the body of Christ: it's distance and indifference that dismember the body, and we are all desperate to stop feeling abandoned and cut off. This is the reality of the body of Christ: selfishness is a form of self-mutilation.

We are all a body, we belong to one another, we are one.

This is the practical reality. Relationship is the only real reality. Unless our everyday reality reflects the practical reality of our oneness, we live a horror story of distortion and dismemberment. To be the re-membering people—this is the work of life in a brokenhearted world.

I look up and the moment is weightless, lifted in a spiral of candle flame underneath the big cross on the wall. *Do this in re-membrance of Me.* Anything less than living out the reality of the oneness of the body is illusion and ends in insanity.

Elizabeth once sent me a paper nativity. The wise men were all still joined. Elizabeth's love for us, it broke the limits of time, broke the limits of her body, her heart. "Sometimes you were publicly exposed to insult and persecution; at other times you *stood side by side* with those who were so treated."[8] The phrase "side by side" translates the Greek *koinonoi*—"companions," "partners." Stand side by side as partners in their sufferings. Participate, get into their suffering, let it make you grimy and tear-stained, and drink the draught of communion.

Koinonia is more than a cup of coffee and small talk; it is the fellowship of the broken sharing brokenness. Somewhere a fan whirs to life. The woman in front of me shifts from foot to foot. The little girl beside me, Lark, sobs into her mother's skirt. Elizabeth had taught her how to knit. Lark had sent Elizabeth hand-drawn cards of hearts with smiling flowers. My hand finds the curve of Lark's shoulder and stays with her.

How do you know how to hold space for all this brokenness and not be afraid? This cross on my wrist—it's been showing me how to hold pain, to hold the pain of little deaths. To not be afraid of it, to not fight it. The cross allows you to hold pain—because that cross is absorbing all your pain.

Oh, Elizabeth, how will I go on without you and I have to

go on without you and I wish I could tell you, say it before the dark falls, that this is who stood at your funeral: the woman in a gray cardigan you wrote birthday cards to and went to her daughter's piano recitals. The man in the wrinkled suit and too-tight tie you called on long after everyone else stopped, the woman in the black dress you gave a second chance to, the kid with the puffy red eyes you forgave when she expected you to walk away. The people who fill the pews at your funeral were those you never stopped persevering with and showing up for and believing in. It's not titles and power in the pews of your funeral; it's your people, your friends and family, your feats of love. All those you broke and gave yourself for and became the gift to, and they bear your gifts and all the love you gave away. And how does your coffin reverberate with the truth of it? *Loving by halves is not how anyone becomes whole.* How do you tell someone before they go—*you have loved me like this?*

Stories of her, all the ways she became the GIFT, are shared at a microphone. A humming peace, something sacred pulses through our veins, enlarging our lungs. It leaks through the beating of our broken hearts: *there are many ways, but there's only one way that leads to life.* The performing way of the world is about impressing people, about creating your own parade of accomplishments. And the cruciform way of Christ is about letting the love of God and the needs of people impress and form you into a cross, being the Samaritan who sacrifices to help the other wounded paraders and upholding the forgotten.

One way leads to a dead end, the other to love. What drives us to try to build a successful life rather than a meaningful life?

Elizabeth poured out her bucket—and she gave the gift of her secret: *a willingness to be inconvenienced is the ultimate proof of love.* This is what dying to live means: You love as much as you are willing to be inconvenienced. Why hadn't I ever seen this before? Those counted wheat seeds at home in their own container, wouldn't they be best invested if I looked for ways to sow them into the broken soil of my own inconvenience? Yes, the best investment of your life is to love *exactly* when it's most inconvenient. If I won't be inconvenienced, I can't know love. Am I willing to live an inconvenient life? The brokenness of people is never truly an intrusion. Loving broken people when it is inconvenient is the way to have fuller inclusion in the life of Christ.

Teach me to number my days, O Lord, that I may gain a heart of wisdom.[9]

The real sinew of community, the muscle of *koinonia*, is not in how well we impress each other, but in how well we inconvenience ourselves for each other. Five pallbearers gather at the front by the stand of lilies. They turn, take their sides, and carry her out. They carry her out by me.

That night when my fears of my kid following in my footsteps loomed like inevitability? Elizabeth had sat up with me, unafraid of my pain, of all the brokenness. She was a GIFTer, never counting on somebody else to show up, because she had known, and had shown me: the people who can be counted on to show up—are the only ones who have something real to show for their life.

I want to go after her draped coffin. I want to *be* her. All of us at Elizabeth's funeral say this when we gather at the cemetery, there at her deep hole in an aching gust of spring: we didn't want to leave. We say we don't want to walk away because she had loved us not in the expected, transactional way, but in this unexpected, transformational way. Elizabeth is part of my transformation. Loss can always be transformative.

"I am certain that I never did grow in grace one half so much anywhere as I have upon the bed of pain," assured Spurgeon.[10] "I am not a theologian or a scholar," Elisabeth Elliot said, "but I am very aware of the fact that pain is necessary to all of us. In my own life, I think I can honestly say that out of the deepest pain has come the strongest conviction of the presence of God and the love of God."[11] The most crushing lie a life can hold on to is that life is supposed to avoid suffering, avoid loss, avoid anything that breaks. Loss is our very air; we, like the certain spring rains, are always falling toward the waiting earth, but we can forget this. We desperately try to forget this. Elizabeth, she remembered, and she showed us how to be broken and given into His waiting arms. Her life was spent in inconvenience, loving so beyond limits that it broke our hearts, testifying here in a windswept cemetery. Loving people without expecting anything in return always turns out to have the greatest returns.

Elizabeth escapes in the spring rains, crosses over like a robin, a flutter of wings just past the edge of our view, singing of lovely things coming that then fly away and are gone. I pick up a single petal from one of the white roses that has blown off her casket. I hold it as we drive out of the cemetery, passing by her one last time.

On the way home, a man named Lorne looks like he needs help finding his way. I stop, ask how I can help. He shows me the name of what he's looking for, asks me the time. His face is a dawning light of realization in me when he nods good-bye.

I take an extra minute later to tell a cashier how she's gold medaling in service with a smile. Her eyes shimmer, instantly familiar. I stop and whisper to a kid reading a book on a street bench—readers like her are the next world changers—and I wait for the light. I get to be the gift still, to give it forward, to break and give away all the love Elizabeth gave to me. I look into the eyes of people all the way home. And for a string of moments, I remember that I get to live into the dare that though there is suffering in this world, though there is dying of the loveliest and most loved, though shards of our broken hearts pierce our lungs' every breath, there's the grace of a miraculous communion of all the broken. There's the dare to come to the feast to be shared.

"Faith is a living, daring confidence in God's grace, so sure and certain that a man could stake his life on it a thousand times," penned Martin Luther.[12] This life is a dare to break and give away God's grace a thousand times, to stake your life on His grace a thousand times over, to live endless little cruciform deaths—until we fly away and are gone from here.

I get home later, deeply grieving and more deeply fulfilled, and find a pen and re-ink that cross into skin.

It's never too late to live a remarkable, inconvenient life given to the interruptions of now.

That is what love is too: Love is the willingness to be interrupted. *Interrupt* comes from the Latin word *interrumpere*, meaning "break into." *Love is the willingness to be broken into.* There are never interruptions in a day—only manifestations of Christ. Your theology is best expressed in your availability and your interruptability—and ability to be broken into. This is the broken way. This is all love. And I hadn't known—I will only love as well as I let myself be broken into.

Would she ever know how I'd just wanted to tell her, "Before the day of your funeral ended, I got home in time to pour the seeds of wheat from the tin bucket back into the Mason jar. I set it there on the windowsill beside the folded rose petal, your last gift to me—though your life would keep giving me endless gifts, but I didn't know that yet. And the only sound breaking the silence in that moment as I stood there was the old ticking clock—but I heard it different this time, with hope that might embrace even the inconvenient things, because you lived like you did. Because you lived breaking into each new moment"?

Because you actually lived.

Fourteen

Breaking the Lies
in Your Head

He went without comfort so you might have it. He postponed joy so you might share in it. He willingly chose isolation so you might never be alone in your hurt and sorrow.

JONI EARECKSON TADA

The soil in the garden feels warm under my knees. I can't stop thinking about her. How Elizabeth's laugh sounded like the rain of childlike laughter and I'm parched. *Do the next thing. When nothing feels simple, simply do the next thing.* "You don't judge your feelings. You simply feel your feelings." My friend turns those words over to me on the phone like an unearthing, an excavating of something sacred. "That's what feelings are for—feeling."

I'd been bent down in the garden. Pulling out a bunch of overwintered, dead kale plants. Cradling the phone between my shoulder and my ear, listening to the words:

"You don't judge your feelings; you feel feelings—*and then give them to God.*"

I stop. Straighten. Something overwintered in me, something frozen numb and dead, breaks open through the hardened earth. Elizabeth's body's been lying in the ground three weeks now. She's not coming back, ever, and this isn't a bad dream I can ever wake up from. Her voice has flown from the earth.

I have to go. I have to get off the phone. I have to breathe. It's all I can do to stammer out a good-bye, drop the phone softly on the mossy brick walkway, and breathe.

What if I began to feel? What if I let the dam of feelings break? It was coming, and there was no stopping it. Grieving how plans change—is part of the plan to change us. Elizabeth had broken something in me; she'd broken me open to this reaching out to trace the face of suffering, to feel along its features—and I hadn't wanted to recoil, but at times, it felt too much, too vulnerable, to live broken into life like that. But what if I didn't recoil from this? What if I didn't pull back from the pain?

What happens if you just let the brokenness keep coming? Surrender. Let the wave of it all break over you and wash you up at the foot of that cross. What if I lived like I believed it: *Never be afraid of broken things—because Christ is redeeming everything.*

Elizabeth is gone. And I've failed to love like I've wanted to. Always, I'd about give my eye teeth and left arm for more time to get it more deeply right and less painfully wrong. I wanted to be more—more patient, to never lose it, to always have it together, to keep calm and sane. I've wanted more flashes of wisdom in the heat of the moment when I had no bloody idea what was the best thing to do. I've wanted fewer nights crawling into bed feeling like a failure who always gets it wrong when everyone else seems to get it right. I've wanted to take the gold medal in living well and loving large and being enough to be wanted. Instead, I've been the person who escapes behind bathroom doors, the person who turns on the water so no one can hear the howl, the person who fights what is and struggles to surrender, who completely ups and forgets how to break into givenness. And there's the razor edge of it: I am not someone who once walked nice and neat on this narrow way, and then suddenly didn't. I'm not someone who just tripped and stumbled a bit, but then pulled herself back up on the narrow path. I'm the person who's always been shattered on the inside, knowing brokenness deep in the marrow and ache of me, the one who has wasted days, years, despairing and replaying the past, who's let lies live loud in my head, held grudges, and grown bitter, who's cut myself down, literally, and known depression, suicidal and self-sabotaging self-destruction, and been convinced she would so keenly feel like a broken failure in the end that she'd wish she had never been born.

Feelings of failure can be like this bad rash—scratch one failure and all you can see is an outbreak spreading all over you. Can I choke it out, how this trying to love, how this surrendering to being cruciform—which is what love is—can feel like being lashed to an altar and your bare back stinging a bit raw? How there are times you'd like to cut and break free and run, only to realize you'd be running into meaninglessness—which would only hurt and break you more. What if you just want desperately, in spite of everything, for someone to remember how hard you've really tried? There are days when the sharp edge of self-condemnation cuts you so deep that you can be reaching, grasping, but can't seem to remember to believe that He believes in you. *God, make us the re-membering people.*

Maybe the only way to begin breaking free is to lay open your willing hands and bear witness to the ugly mess of your scars. To trace them slowly and re-member what He says about you, even if you forget. This is about bravely letting our darkness be a canvas for God's light. *This happened that the glory of God might be shown through even you.*[1] What if the re-membering of your brokenness comes in remembering that your trying isn't what matters the most, because His scars have written your name and your worth over all of yours?

Kneeling on the garden path, sun on my neck, in a brown and dead patch of brittle kale, I keep tracing the outline of the bricks, finding a way. There's this breaking, this spilling for all that hasn't been. All that I haven't been. The lament and the grieving and the repentance all mingle. Feelings are meant to be fully felt and then fully surrendered to God. The word *emotion* comes from the Latin for "movement"—and all feelings are meant to move you toward God.

What if I fully surrendered to becoming cruciform so I could feel along my scars, along my own scarred face, and know my own name is Beloved? I don't know if there's any other way to break into abundant living unless I come to *know* this.

All this failing rises from the ground of the kitchen garden toward heaven, bits of dead kale leaves breaking and falling in hardly a whisper of wind. The garden path bricks feel like a kind beckoning forward under my tracing fingertips, my bent knees.

I don't turn away—grief can feel like an aching love song.

It's after the kale has crumbled and this grief has rattled the windows with the wind, after the calcification around the heart's broken and split away, after I've shut my eyes and drowned a bit, that Hope comes into our room, throws herself across the foot of the bed, and I can see the girl's just looking for a way to stand.

"So . . . what exactly am I supposed to do now, Mama?" And

I know she means about friends who betray and break trust, I know that before she even finishes . . . Girls can be downright mean and women can devour each other and Christians can crucify each other and I just keep telling my girl that: Girls can rival each other, but real women revive each other, girls can impale each other, but real women empower each other. Girls can compare each other, but real women champion each other and we are all made to be ground breakers and peace makers and freedom shakers.

I sit across from Hope, memorizing her face. My girl and I are mirrors of each other, mirrors of the same kind of different. When you lose someone or when people steal something of you, you're left trying to find yourself again. We're all in the midst of our own identity crises, trying to find our own busted way.

Someone's left a light on down the hallway.

"Really, it's all going to be okay." I try to tell this to her, to me. "We're going to be okay—even if we feel un-okay." Can I remember to let feelings be fully felt and then fully surrendered to God? Emotions are given to move you toward God. Can I remember? I don't have to fix things, I don't have to deny things, I don't have to pretend away things. Could I simply feel the brokenness of things—and feel that's okay? Could I feel okay being un-okay, trusting that Christ is always making a way?

Hope puts her head in my lap. I gather her long hair in my hands, gather her mane all in one long strand and twist it slow, around and around, as if I can somehow make a rope for my girl, for us, to hold on to.

"Hope-girl, listen. . . ." A robin trills out in the sunburst locust at the corner of the house. "If we all listen long enough to the voices about who we should be, we grow deaf to the beauty of who we are."

My throat hurts. *How long can we be deaf to our own words?* Her hair feels like long silk between my fingers.

A cacophony of voices about who you should be or how you are supposed to feel or how you have to do this and that to be good enough, and you still don't measure up—it can feel like a dark serpentine shadow suffocating you. A death-squeeze around the two of us. The robin falls silent.

When you're most wounded by the world—run to the only Word that brings healing.

And His Word makes it clear: at the core of every one of our issues is this attempt to construct our identity on something else besides Christ.

Hadn't Søren Kierkegaard described sin as not to will to be oneself before God—to "be in despair at not willing to be oneself"—and faith as "that the self in willing to be itself is grounded transparently in God"?[2] You are most who you are meant to be when no wind in the world can stop you from being grounded transparently in God. You are your truest self when you live with your heart as glass to God.

"Sin is the despairing refusal to find your deepest identity in your relationship and service to God," writes theologian Tim Keller. "Sin is seeking to become oneself, to get an identity, apart from him. What does this mean? Everyone gets their identity, their sense of being distinct and valuable, from somewhere or something . . . Human beings were made not only to believe in God in some general way, but to love him supremely, center their lives on him above anything else, and build their very identities on him. Anything other than this is sin."[3]

What I won't break to build my identity on Him is sin.

Everything falls quiet. Hope's long and willowy next to me, like a stilled sapling leaning, looking for light. And I'm looking for words to give her what I know of the scars and history of my own brokenness: you can't experience intimacy with Christ until you know your identity in Christ. Activity for God—is not the same as intimacy with God or identity in God. And it is your intimacy with Christ that gives you your identity. You can't experience the power of Christ, the mission of Christ, being made new in Christ, until you know who you are in Christ. Your identity literally means "the same"—that regardless of changing circumstances, the core of you is unchangeable, stable, the same.

When your identity is in Christ, your identity is the same yesterday, today, and tomorrow. Criticism can't change it. Failing can't shake it. Lists can't determine it. When your identity is in the Rock, your identity is rock-solid. As long as God is for you, it doesn't matter what mountain rises ahead of you. You aren't your yesterday, you aren't your messes, you aren't your failures, you aren't your brokenness. You are brave enough for today, because He is. You are strong enough for what's coming, because He is. And you are enough for all that is, *because He always is.*

Nothing can break your life like not knowing who you are in Christ, and there is nothing that needs breaking more in life than the lies about who you are in Christ. The greatest danger to our soul is not success or status or superiority—but self-lies. When you listen to the self-lies hissing that you're unlovable, unacceptable, unwanted, that's when you go seeking your identity in success or status or superiority and not in your Savior. Self-lies are the destroyer of the soul because they drown out the sacred voice that can never stop whispering your name: *Beloved.*

"Hope." She turns her face. I can start here. I can tell it slant. I can meet her brokenness with bits of my own because the shortest distance between two hearts is always the way of brokenness. "I ever tell you about when my uncle Paul started chasing me through the house with that snake?"

She rolls onto her back across our bed, her searching eyes finding mine. "He chased you with a snake?"

I stroke her hair slow, my girl trying to navigate the words and feelings of broken people with serrated edges that cut her deep.

"I mean, he didn't mean anything by it. Uncle Paul, he'd turn out the lights in Gram's yellow-tiled kitchen. Then he'd flick on the flashlight and spin it round till the light was flooding up this glossy two-page spread from one of Great-Grandpa's old *National Geographic*s. And for a little kid, that paper snake was as real as if its sandpaper tongue had licked me."

I can still close my eyes and see it, that beady-eyed snake with its mouth wide. You can spend your one wild life trying to outrun glossy, beady-eyed lies, the fears strangling you right there at your thin neck.

"One of the devil's greatest weapons is to make you believe you're all alone," I tell her. "You are not alone." And we're never alone in feeling alone. We've all felt as if we're unwanted failures and it's Jesus who cups our faces close: "I'll never let you down, never walk off and leave you."[4]

"In grade school, Josie Miller said I must be wearing clothes from the bottom of some garbage bag from the Sally Ann because I was a rotting, musty mess that stunk up the world."

I lean in close to Hope.

"People will always have opinions about you. But you live for God because He's the only one who has intimate knowledge of you. Nothing anyone says can malign you, assign you, or confine you. Your Maker's the only one who can define you. Your identity isn't founded on you finding yourself. Feelings

NEVER BE AFRAID

OF BROKEN THINGS—

BECAUSE CHRIST

IS REDEEMING

EVERYTHING.

are meant to be felt and given to God—but feelings can't tell you about God, you, or your relationship. Your identity, your security, your acceptability come from who God is—and not how you feel. Because there was something before what you felt about yourself—and that is what God feels about you. Feelings are meant to be felt and then taken to God, who felt first about you. Will you believe first how He feels about you? When you experience how God knows and receives you, you bond with God, united, and let Him speak your true identity and there's nothing more important in this world than to truly feel and know what God feels about you."

Hope's nodding slow, and her finger traces that cross drawn on my wrist.

"And you know what?" I whisper it quietly to Hope, remembering what it was like to be exactly where she is, which seems like its own kind of miraculous *koinonia*. "Whatever Josie Miller thought I smelled of? It wasn't a garbage bag. I'd fed a couple hundred squealing hogs before I ever stepped foot in that school. My hands would smell of hogs and feed troughs and shoveling out pens. There was no getting rid of that smell." How do you become ashamed of who you are? No matter how hard you scrub, it can feel too late to change who you've become. That lie of ugliness and less-than-enoughness slithered under the layers of years and snaked up me a bit.

I pull Hope close. "None of us are ever alone. When I was ten and the school bus dropped me off, I was walking up our farm lane, wearing my red cropped pants with a scent of hog on my hands, when a baseball smashed into the back of my head, and the whole busload of kids erupted in cheers. I turned and saw Lissa Turscott, and I just wanted to die."

"Oh," Hope's eyes read sympathy.

"And in eighth grade, the girls jeered that no one in the whole school was more hated than I was. I can still hear them laughing." I take her hand, bring mine up to her cheek. "But none of us are ever really alone."

I've made wide berths around women for years and skirted the communion of community because who knew when smiles could turn into fangs if you turned your back? Your identity might be broken by lies. And my girl looks like she knows bites that have broken the skin. My fourth-grade teacher, Mrs. Munford, once wagged her finger in my face and said I wasn't smart enough for her class: "You only made it in here by the skin of your teeth, Little Miss Ann, and don't you ever forget it." All my life I've felt like a fraud with skin on.

And what I don't know how to tell her is that later in some way, those words formed me.

They've become like my own name engraved right into me. *Fraud. Phony. Not Good Enough.*

Hope's resting her fingers on my wrist-drawn cross. Some wounds so twist and form us they become more than scars, but who we actually believe we are. Some wounds cut so deep we carry them like our very names. When I'd told my friend Mei what Mrs. Munford had said, she had let me sit with my words, and I'd turned to her and mumbled it, finding my stumbling: "Maybe we all find it easier, safer, to feel like broken misfits than to face the fact that we're beloved. That we belong."

I let my one hand pause in Hope's hair. My pulse beats at my cross-marked wrist, resting on hers.

Living as one truly loved and cherished by God is the crossbeam that supports an abundant life in Christ. Belovedness is the center of being, the only real identity, God's *only* name for you, the only identity He gives you. And you won't ever feel like you belong anywhere until you choose to listen to your heart beating out that you do—unconditionally, irrevocably. Until you let yourself feel the truth of that—the truth your heart has always known because He who made it wrote your name right there.

The clock's ticking loud above the stairs. Hope's tracing the penned cross, and I quietly trace the veins on the back of her hand, like we're both looking for ways.

"I've done more than you will ever know to break myself." She's seen the scars on my wrists. She understands. She's looked into my eyes and seen me. I'm sitting there looking into her.

The mirror her dad and I bought with a little clutch of wedding money, we found it covered in a layer of dust in McFarley's barn full of antiques—it's hanging on the wall across from our bed. There's a tin cross from Haiti hanging beside it. Hope and I look wavy in the old glass.

Something in me hurts deep—because your girl can mirror you. I can't stop reading her eyes. *Don't judge the feelings. Feelings are meant to be felt . . . and then surrender the feelings to God. God, I don't want her to hurt.* I don't want her to hurt alone. I don't want her to feel broken alone. I want to share in her sufferings, participate in her sufferings. The worst human emotion to experience is aloneness. And I want *koinonia* with her, want her to feel it—the brokenness and givenness of *koinonia* is always worth the risk. I want to cup her face in my hands and tell her, tell both of us: that serpent, the enemy of your soul, his name means "prosecutor" and that's what he does—he tries to make you feel alone and on trial, tries to make your life a trial to get you to prosecute yourself. He poisons you endlessly with self-lies. And the first tactic of the enemy of your soul is always to distort your identity. You can feel the hiss slithering up your neck like this deafening replay in your head: *Did God really say you were worth anything? Look at you—you're damaged goods. You're too broken to be chosen.*

That's the voice that rattles me, that can form my feelings, that too often can shape my identity instead of the cross, that keeps me lying awake night after night, fearing I've run out of time, fearing I've missed the boat, fearing I was never good enough for the "real boat," fearing I'll probably get kicked off this boat. *Surrender the feelings. Break open your heart and honestly feel and surrender the feelings to God.* In the middle of the night, sometimes you can hear Him in your heart beating out His truth to the lying prosecutor and all these fears: *You've never missed any boat when you're holding on to the cross.*

Hope curls into me. I'm desperate to make her self-lies go away. Hers. Mine. *God, help.*

Isn't the fear that I am not enough really the lie that God isn't enough?

If every belittling of self is a belittling of God, a kind of blaspheming of God's sufficiency and enoughness, then maybe . . . maybe we don't really have faith until we have faith that God loves us right now more than we could ever dream of loving ourselves.

What if speaking your most unspoken broken is what it takes to release a dammed-up Niagara Falls of grace? Grace that says your faith doesn't have to try to measure up to anyone else because Jesus came down—and He measures you as good enough, as worthy enough, as loved more than enough. Grace embraces you before you prove anything, and after you've done everything wrong. Every time you fall down, at the bottom of every hole is grace. Grace waits in broken places. Grace waits at the bottom of things. Grace loves you when you are at your darkest worst, and wraps you in the best light. Grace seeps through the broken places and seeps into the lowest places, a balm for wounds.

That's the tragedy and the comedy of life: Grace is grace when it gives us what we'd never ask for but always needed, and moves us to become what we always wanted. *But hardly ever the way we wanted*.

I uncoil Hope's long hair from my fingers. It falls free. Touch her cheek.

Grace is what holds you when everything's breaking and falling apart, and whispers that everything is really falling together.

She closes her eyes.

A simple line of words can be a lifeline. Words can be the essence of the ministry of presence. "That is what we've always got to do," I whisper, "what you and I and all the broken can never stop doing: *shake off that lying snake and break free*." Because that lying snake's head's been long crushed. No, make that pulverized. For the love, and for the sake of God, let go of the self-lies. It's in a frame on the wall over my desk: "Is not this thing in my right hand a lie?"[5]

It's only when you know your real identity that you can really break the enemy and break free. No matter what you've lost or who you've lost, or what bits of you have been broken off and lost—nothing that's happened in the past can change it, and nothing in the future can intimidate the reality of it, because this is the realest true: you are always sufficient because God always gives you His all-sufficient grace.

I press my hand into Hope's, my wrist and its drawn cross into her wrist, like the gift of who He is can be imprinted right into her.

Some kid slams the back door too loud on his way in. That tin cross falls off its pin on the wall beside the dresser. Hope leans over the edge of the bed, picks it up off the floor, and hands it to me.

It was once a discarded oil barrel. Now it's cut and hammered into the shape of a cross. Like it's a sign: *How we are is not who we are. How we feel about us is not how He feels about us.* "All His is mine and all mine"—my sins, my death, my damnation—"is His," writes Luther.[6] *How we are is not who we are. Who we are is who He is.*

The tin cross in my hand mirrors the ink cross on my wrist. The world and us, we are all being re-formed. Union with Christ—this is how to be fully human. Union with Christ, writes Karl Barth, "is the starting-point for everything else to be thought and said concerning what makes the Christian a Christian."[7] Believers in Christ are seen by God exactly as Christ is seen by God. *I am who He is.* I am crucified with Christ, unified with Christ, identified with Christ. *Full stop. Full story. I am who He is.* I am not the mistakes I have made; I am the righteousness He has made. I am not the plans I have failed; I am the perfectness He has finished. I am not the wrongs I have done; I am the faultlessness He has been. I am not the sins I have chosen; I am chosen by the Beloved, *regardless of my sins*. In Christ, I am chosen, accepted, justified, anointed, sealed, forgiven, redeemed, complete, free, Christ's friend, God's child, Spirit's home.

The cross, this is the sign of who I am, of my actual and realest identity. Maybe all the brokenhearted don't need to try to believe more in themselves, but to believe what Jesus says about them more. Your value is not defined by your achievements. Your value is defined by the One who said, "It is finished!" and who *achieved it all*. You don't have to be awesome and do everything; you simply have to believe that the One who is truly awesome loves you through everything.

You're more than your hands do.

You're more than your hands have.

You're more than how other hands measure you.

You are what is written on God's hands: *Safe. Held. His. Beloved.*

"Yeah, Mama . . ." Hope gently squeezes my hand. "I think I hear what you're saying—that once you face Him, you see who you really are . . . so you can go face anything."

That—exactly that.

Be brave. Your bravery wins a thousand battles you can't see because your bravery strengthens a thousand others to win their battles too.

I run my fingers around the edge of the cross. The tin's got all these hammered indentations, raised spots like braille around these depressions. And it's in the depressions of feeling not enough that we have to say, *"Enough!"* to the lies: *"Is not this thing in my right hand a lie?"*[8]

Hope's hand lies in mine. *Break the lies. Break the self-lies.* I can feel her pulse. We both breathe together slow. The caress of God meets us in a stillness on the inside. It's when we let the lies grow so loud around us and in us that we forget how to live from the inside out. Old barrels can forget they are being formed into crosses. *Identity formation is most complete when we are formed like a cross.* I slip the cross back into Hope's hand. When love's got ahold of you—there isn't a lie in the universe that can pull you apart.

"Careful." I smile at her standing there smiling at me, certain and brave. "The edge of that cross is sharp." There's a cross that can be a weapon in your hand. There's a cross you can take into your heart to break you free . . .

. . . that can cut the head off a lying snake.

Fifteen

How to Be an Esther and Break a Thousand Gates

*Christians who understand biblical truth and
have the courage to live it out can indeed redeem a
culture, or even create one.*

CHUCK COLSON

If you only knew what fire every person is facing, there isn't one fire you wouldn't help fight with the heat of a greater love.

The day the homeless man moved into our loft, a heat wave broke over us.

Gordon literally had nothing the day he showed up, nothing to his name but the sun-faded T-shirt sticking to his back, emblazoned with the words, "Normal people scare me." A mingling of alcohol and tobacco seeps from his burning pores. My brother and a buddy, they'd found him wandering down an empty back road after a court date, the tongues of his boots panting open, longing for relief. Now he stands in the shade at our back door, asking for water.

"You got anything to drink?" he asks me.

My brother wonders if we have some work for Gordon. Wondered if we may have a place for him, and maybe—just to start—a glass of water?

Gordon uses the tattered edge of his T-shirt to mop this mask of sweat puddling in the etched lines of his face. A silver cross hangs around his neck on this heavy chain. Before I even think, I touch my wrist to find the small black cross I penned first thing this morning. *We both have our crosses. We all have our crosses.* "To be a follower of the Crucified means, sooner or later, a personal encounter with the cross. And the cross always entails loss," writes Elisabeth Elliot.[1]

The sun's losing light as it edges across the floor.

I can feel the world tilting a bit, its truth slipping right out and onto the floor between Gordon and me: Why do we rush to defend God to a broken world, and not race to defend the image of God in the world's broken? Gordon's eyes search mine. The light's caught in his hair. Yeah, I've got no idea if he's packing something, dealing something, trafficking something, but something holy's caught in my throat. *We've all got our crosses.*

Maybe the struggle for good isn't waged as much around us as it's waged inside of us. I could get Gordon a glass of water. Could I offer him a place to stay? Why in the world do we spend more time defending God to the critical around us than defending God to the doubting, critical voices within us? What if it is not God who needs us to rush to His defense in the world as much as we need to rush to the distress of the broken who carry the image of God into the world?

I think of Queen Esther, the young Jewish girl who found herself a Persian queen when her people faced genocide— Esther, right where she was, *for such a time as this*, to give a glass of cold water, a desperate hand to another, to open a door, a hand, a heart, and give her life away.

This man is standing penniless and parched in my kitchen and I've stood in a kitchen of sorts in a dump in Guatemala

City and looked into the whites of kids' eyes eating whatever they could find in piles of rotting refuse, the vultures circling overhead. I've knelt beside a little girl in Uganda who held a bowl in her two hands, held it up for me to see what she'd caught for dinner, those dozens of crawling bugs. In Iraq, I've sat in a cold shipping container with refugee women whose brothers and fathers were shot in front of them by terrorists, women who had to make a split-minute decision which child they could take with them and which would be left behind, women who had nothing, yet offered me their rationed tea and we sat on the floor and wept because shared tears are multiplied healing. And I've stood at a chain-link fence in Haiti when a small boy appeared out of nowhere, the barren foothills bloating malnourished up behind him as he rattled the fence with one dirty hand and pointed to his cracked lips, begging for food—even a sip of water.

And they come again to me now in my kitchen, Esther's cousin's words: "Don't think for a moment that because you're in the palace you will escape when all other Jews are killed. If you keep quiet at a time like this, deliverance and relief for the Jews will arise from some other place, but you and your relatives will die."[2] You can look into eyes and hear the whisper from those outside your door, outside the gate: You've got to risk your position inside for those on the outside or you risk losing everything, even your own soul. You've got to give your gifts or they may become your idols, your identity, and you become the walking dead. If your living isn't about giving, then you're already dying. You've got to use the life you've been given to give others life. If your life isn't about giving relief—you don't get real life. Give relief or you find none. For what does it profit a woman to gain the whole world, but lose her own soul?[3]

You are where you are for such a time as this. Not to gain anything, but to risk everything.

Gordon doesn't need me to beckon more than once and he's in the cool of the house, yanking off those boots. I'm in the kitchen finding a cup. My brother's standing in the doorway, waiting to see whatever's coming. The water streams from the faucet like it can't wait to give itself away and I hold out all our cups for the filling.

I turn, hand Gordon his, one to my brother, and I swallow my own right down. We're all more than a bit parched.

We could all be the ones outside the gate. We all could have been Gordon, fallen on hard times into hard ways; we could have been the one fighting the Lord's Resistance Army slitting our child's throat in the middle of the night; we could be the one born into a slum, violently raped and left for dead, the one born into AIDS, into starvation, into lives of Christ-less desperation. The reason you are inside the gate for such a time as this—is to risk your life for those outside the gate.

If I perish, I perish.

There are so many of us sucking down lattes and dying of thirst, dying for something more, for something abundant. There are so many in need, and so many Esthers who thirst for more than vanilla services, sweetened programs, and watered-down lives, hungry for some real meat for their starved souls, some dirt under the fingernails, some real sacrifice in the veins. I know why I keep writing a cross on my wrist.

There are those who are saved, but only by the skin of their teeth because they cared most about the comfort of their own skin and only minimally about anyone else's. They will have a hardly abundant entrance awaiting them in heaven. But those will not be the Esthers. There are those who would rather turn a blind eye to the needy than turn to the needy and be like Christ. Those who would love playing at being Christian more than actually being one and loving giving. But those will not be the Esthers.

There's a whole generation of Esthers who want to be the gift, want to give it forward, whatever's in our hands, who want holy more than hollow. There's a whole Esther Generation, and it is we who want the abundant life of going lower to love the least, the lonely, and the lost. The world needs people who will defy cynical indifference by making a critical difference.

Every one of us can start changing headlines when we start reaching out our hands.

We can be concerned for the poor—but be no less concerned for us rich who claim not to be rich so we can excuse ourselves from giving. Go ahead and show concern for the poor—but be no less concerned if we've merely done enough to assuage our consciences, just enough to pat ourselves on the back, but not enough that we've ever felt true sacrifice, that we've ever actually *broken* and given. Go ahead and live concerned for the poor—but be no less concerned for avoiding suffering because someday we will face Christ. What if caring for the poor was more than just caring about easing our consciences? What if caring for the poor may mean sacrifice, and what if this is the way to be *satisfied* and know abundant living?

I'd read it once—how one in four people in a small town was deaf. And every one of them felt like an outsider. Until everyone in town learned sign language. The non-deaf disadvantaged themselves, inconvenienced themselves, to learn sign language. And it was the non-deaf whose lives were enhanced in unexpected ways. Not only did they gain rich relationships with deaf neighbors they would have missed out on otherwise, but they also discovered the convenience of signing across the street to one another, of sign language communicating from atop hills to folks below, of the sick signing what they needed when voices failed, of children signing to avoid being loud. Disadvantaging themselves—turned out to be their advantage. *Brokenness was made into abundance.*

"To 'do justice,'" writes Tim Keller, "means to go to places where the fabric of shalom has broken down, where the weaker members of societies are falling through the fabric, and to repair it."[4]

We are each singular threads in the world. We all get to decide what we will tie our lives to. If I tie my resources, my time, my Esther-power, only to the thin thread of my own life—my life's a hopelessly knotted mess.

The thread of your life becomes a tapestry of abundant colors only if it ties itself to other lives. The only way to strengthen the fabric of society is to let threads of your life break away to let Christ, who is in us, weave around other threads. "Reweaving shalom means to sacrificially thread, lace, and press our time, power, goods, and resources into the lives and needs of others . . . The strong must disadvantage themselves for the weak, the majority for the minority, or the community frays and the fabric breaks."[5]

The only way to care for the disadvantaged is to disadvantage yourself, *which is guaranteed to turn out to your advantage.*

What if we gave up charity for solidarity? What if we gave up giving from the top down and gave ourselves in reaching out, less the vertical and more like the horizontal beam of the cross? All on the same beam, all of us in need of the cross, all with our own crosses. We each have our own pack of addictions and predilections, and we're dying for a cold drink to soothe the burning edges of our wounds. For all our masks and pearly smiles, we're a whole world of Gordons.

We've all been the ones outside the gate pleading for Someone to risk everything to rescue us. This could break a million little self-righteous pulpits: *the brokenness in the world is but the brokenness in our own busted hearts.*

My own busted heart's got nothing to give. But I don't need to have things together before I can offer a cup of water, open the door, my hand, or reach out to help those outside. I don't need to not be thirsty myself; I only need to know I thirst too.

Because grace is a beam that begs us to let it run on and support everything.

And it isn't *having* that makes us rich; it's *giving.* Give sacrificially, live richly. Maybe all we really want is more of God. Abundance of Him.

Gordon's sitting here with no place to lay his head: "Despised and rejected by men; a man of sorrows, and acquainted with grief; and as one from whom men hide their faces he was despised."[6] "When you bring a cup of cold water to the least of these, you bring it to Me."[7] I fill his glass again with deep-well water and he drains the cup dry, slams it on the counter, and grins a country-mile wide.

"I was a stranger and you welcomed Me," I hear.[8] *Oh, my God. I could have missed You.*

How many times have I missed Him? You miss Him when you question who's needy enough to give to, who warrants the risk. He comes as the homeless guy, the refugee, the child drinking filthy water—and you get to decide. Are you going to fill your life with more stuff, more safety, or more God? What the world says is weak and small may be where Christ is offering Himself to you most of all—and why do we want to be big people when God shows up as the little people nobody's got time for? You miss Jesus when you aren't looking for His two disguises: the smallest and the servant.

"The mystery of ministry is that the Lord is to be found where we minister," writes Henri Nouwen. "That is what Jesus tells us when He says: 'Insofar as you did this to one of the least of these brothers of mine, you did it to me' (Matthew 25:40). Our care for people thus becomes the way to meet the Lord. The more we give, support, guide, counsel and visit, the more we receive, not just similar gifts, but the Lord Himself. To go to the poor is to go to the Lord."[9]

I get back from Iraq, where I sat with women who witnessed genocide, and at church somebody tells me, "It's nice that you care about those people over there." And I stop. Turn. How do I translate it? We aren't where we are to care about those on the margins—some nice gesture or token concern. I look across the kitchen at Gordon. The reason we are here is to risk everything for those oppressed people *over there* outside the gate. You are where you are to help others where they are. This isn't a Christian's sideline hobby; compassion is our complete vocation. We do not just care about people; caring is our calling. That's it.

God forbid, you don't get a roof over your head and food on your table because you deserve more, but so you can serve more. God forbid, you believe you're a little better than others instead of making another's life a little better. Gordon's voice crackles like it's been scorched: "So, I know that your brother, you and he have talked?" My brother had texted me before they arrived. "You think I could crash here for a bit?"

"Yeah, Gordon." The words spill out before I'm really thinking, trying to get the invitation out before reservations. "We've got an extra bed up in the loft . . ."

THE ONLY WAY

TO CARE FOR THE DISADVANTAGED

IS TO DISADVANTAGE YOURSELF,

WHICH IS GUARANTEED

TO TURN OUT TO YOUR ADVANTAGE.

I could hear the cautions in my head: Is this safe? *But what is love if not this? Real love is never safe.* When it comes to real love, there is safety in danger. How many times have I thought it was safety that mattered, when Jesus already died to save us? No one ever got saved unless someone else was willing to be unsafe. Some notion of safety isn't what ultimately matters; what matters is: *If we see someone in need and don't help in some way, isn't that in some way sin?* Love of strangers—wasn't that the direct, exact translation of the word for hospitality in Scripture, *philoxenia*? *Philos*—brotherly love; *xenia*—the stranger. Love the stranger like a brother. Biblical hospitality is about inviting strangers in, not just the neighbors.

Jesus feels loud in the space between Gordon and me and so easily unheard at the same time:

> "When you give a lunch or a dinner, don't invite your friends, your brothers, your relatives, or your rich neighbors, because they might invite you back, and you would be repaid. On the contrary, when you host a banquet, invite those who are poor, maimed, lame, or blind. And you will be blessed, because they cannot repay you."[10]

Give the gift forward to the stranger who cannot repay you, to those outside the gate, so the only repayment is the abundance of God. The sun's spilling down the old wooden barn ladder I'd placed by the kitchen table. Grace is always a movement of downward mobility.

The world changes when we don't categorize, polarize, and demonize people with broad brushstrokes—but when we apologize, empathize, evangelize, and prioritize people with these quiet brushes of grace.

Gordon pushes back the stool, stands, leans into the counter. "Think you might have work for me? Cause I'm hard up for cash like you wouldn't believe." His appeal falls into the dusk's quiet. Can the one who appeals—always look the most appealing? Isn't this the broken heart of Christ? Some questions you can't answer theologically, but only with your life.

"Sure, Gordon." I catch his eye. "Pretty sure we've got some work for you."

Faces are mirrors that prove all our separateness is mirage.

All there is to see is Jesus. All there is to see is the face of Jesus in others—and for them to see the face of Jesus in you. Wasn't that it? Seeing Jesus' presence in others is the secret to becoming *like His presence* to others. Maybe you can only be Christ in the world to the extent that *you see Christ's presence in the world.* And we only refuse to be like Christ to each other—when we refuse to see Christ in each other.

In my periphery, I can see my brother nodding. And when Gordon turns just the least in the dying light, you can see God through brokenness. It strikes me that sight is only possible if light can *break* into us. Refuse light to break into you, and you will walk blind. Refuse to let oxygen break into your lungs, and you will die. *Refuse to let Him break into you, and you will die.* Koinonia is the breaking in, the willing participation, the fellowship of all things—and indwelling can't help but weave its way through all of the atoms of the world. The whole earth is full of His indwelling. The broken way illuminates the whole material world, everything breaking into everything else.

This is what love means: we live within each other, we inhabit each other, our love for each other becoming *stego*, a sheltering roof. Maybe we don't live abundantly until we let the Gordons break into us—the foster child who needs a break, the angry teenager, the guy we can't stand, the neighbor who is always complaining, the people on the other side of the gate, till everyone who crosses your path breaks a bit into your heart. Their vulnerabilities become ours, their prayers become ours, their hopes become ours. Love bears all things and we are the Esthers who bear *whatever it takes* for those outside the gate.

"How 'bout I go get clean sheets for that bed up in the loft for you? And you can hang your hat here for as long as you need to, Gordon."

My brother leans in to ask Gordon what else he needs right now, and I go look for folded sheets in the linen closet. We all began enfolded, we all swam in an indwelling of communion, us indwelling another human being and her indwelling us—her blood and ours too. Before we were ever visible in community, right from the beginning, we were already present in community. *Koinonia* is our literal genesis. Loneliness is illusion. "Loneliness is the nucleus of psychiatry"—the "central core of [the patient's] illness," Dutch psychiatrist J. H. van den Berg wrote.[11] Souls were made to connect to other souls and gates were made to be destroyed—and if we perish, we perish. And to the extent that we find ourselves disconnected, our own souls break into pieces. The whole universe confirms it, rings with it: there is no reality apart from relationship. Reality is exchange, interchange, connection—*koinonia*. Communion is a cross—a mutual intersection. One person's trajectory is intersected by another's journey, and each receives the other's into their own broken places. Which is to say, we become cruciform.

We become the cross. We incarnate Christ. Reality is the cross where the broken meet. Where the refugee and the elderly, the special needs and the desperately needy, the poor in spirit and the remade in Christ—where all the broken intersect and meet and cross paths. The Father breaks open to make room in Himself for the Son, the Son for the Spirit, the Spirit for the Son and the Father: "None of the persons seeks his own; none seeks to know himself in isolation. Irreducibly different as they are, they are entangled in an eternal knot of perfect communion," writes Peter Leithart.[12]

And none of us seek our own and there are no other people's children, no other people's homeless brother, no other people's crisis. We belong to each other because we all mutually indwell each other, and there is nothing worth having inside the gate when we've got pieces of ourselves outside the gate. When we leave people on the other side of the gate—*we lose parts of ourselves.* That's why the Esther Generation risks everything for those outside the gate—because they hold the necessary pieces of our collective soul, *which we need for shalom. Wholeness.* Unless we rise as the Esther Generation and risk everything for those outside the gate—we *will* perish. Guaranteed.

There are pancakes for a late dinner. Gordon and the Farmer and I sit, and Malakai brings stacks of his pancakes to our waiting plates. Our theology is best expressed in our hospitality. Hospitality is living broken-wide-open, living like a roof, a door wide open, a gate destroyer. Right theology is ultimately hospitality that lives broken right open—with your time and your space and your heart. Every day you can do one thing that you wish you could do for everyone. We will be known for our actual fruits, not the intentions of our imaginations.

Hope lights candles. The dog sleeps on the porch in the glow of the lights, there by the dining room window.

The way to slowly die is to believe you live in a space of scarcity and not abundance of generosity. The abundant way to life is the paradox of the broken way, to believe we live with enough time, enough resources, enough God. Any fear of giving to God's kingdom is flawed. It would be like a farmer who feared losing his bucket of seeds so he failed to plant his own field—and thus forfeited the joy of overflowing his barns with the harvest.

From the table, you can see the Mason jar of wheat seeds in the windowsill. There's always enough abundance and grace to risk everything for those in need, because you have the favor of the King and it's only by abundant grace that any of us are here—and if there's abundant grace for us, by God, there's abundant grace for all of us.

I look at Gordon. Radical love isn't as much about where you move to as letting Jesus move you wherever you are—to see Him where He is waiting for you to break the gate and let Him in. He may move you to Africa—or across the street—or He may move you to get a glass of water. But if the love of Christ moves you, it will move you out into the world to break down a thousand common gates. He means for you to live the shalom of communion. Living the broken way, it isn't about where you live; it's about how you love. It's who we love.

"So ya think we can work on that barn roof tomorrow?" The Farmer nods toward Gordon. Gordon, head down in his stack of pancakes, gives a thumbs-up.

"You sure make good pancakes, Kai," I tell the boy. I had no idea what we were having for dinner, hours too late. But Kai has met me, gifted Him forward today, sheltered me in my own uncertain mess of brokenness, with a plate of steaming pancakes, and a warmer presence. He grins, braces gleaming in the candlelight. There are a thousand ways to be welcomed into communion.

A candle in the center of the table flickers out. Hope leans one of the candles to it, relights it. One candle can light a thousand and is in no way diminished—but actually resurrects in a thousand ways.

The only life worth living is the life you lose.

The reflection of candlelight in the window looks like the rising of a thousand flaming Esthers, breaking out of gates and into light.

Sixteen

When It Comes to Wooing
God and Healing Wounds

*Somewhere you begin to discover life when you
fall sick . . . when you're closer to death—then you
realize "I need you, I need people who trust me,
I need people who love me" . . . Most of the time
to discover new meaning we have to go through a
crisis, we have to go through a breakdown.*

JEAN VANIER

"Tell me you went for a walk with her today?" Mei asks me the question like only a friend can, like it's a taunt, like it's a beat-up, stubborn prayer.

"Yes, I asked her. Yes, she said yes. Yes, we went for a walk in the woods today. Showed up and gave the kid the gift of presence—that's all I got." *Make the ever-present Christ present.*

"And?" Mei's asking me like she's trying to take the temperature of my heart. "How'd it go?"

I wrap my hands tight around my steaming mug of green tea like I can warm life into anesthetized places.

"And? And the walk was . . . fine. It was pedestrian."

I wink, Mei frowns. And then I stop. Masks can be garishly embarrassing things.

"Really, it was fine." I flail. "We walked through the woods and the dogs barreled through inches of leaves like they were hunting down some poor creature and it was a regular three-ring circus and a gong show with a bit of glory thrown in—see? Fine."

"And?" She knows. How in the name of all things holy does she always know?

"And then, yeah—it really wasn't." I look down at the green tea, drink the hot down like it could light me with courage. "The whole thing dissolved when I told her we should turn back toward the road. And she was pretty adamant the road was straight ahead, and I was pretty darn sure it wasn't, but I told her, 'Hey, sure, let's go your way, I'm up for the adventure.'"

I set my mug down.

"And then her trail stopped down by the marsh. And she turned around, and I told her the road was back to the west . . . but she didn't head west—she marched directly *south*."

Mei tilts her head, frowns quizzically.

"And yeah, so I stood there stupidly pointing west, and she stopped and turned around in a tangle of thorn bushes and then she said—what I didn't expect. She said, 'What do you know about making any place safe at all? Do you know anything at all about making a safe place for anyone's heart?'"

I'd stood there dumbfounded, unsure what crumbling black hole I'd stepped in. It was like the wind whipped around and there was no air left in the whole burning cavity of my lungs.

I don't mention how I froze like an idiot with my hand still pointing west, thinking I knew the way when obviously, clearly, I did not—not the way that mattered, not the way that connected hearts the way I wanted to, not the way that could suture broken places like I ached to.

"Do you?" She'd yelled it at me like she'd pulled back a bow and released.

Sometimes it helps in the moment to think: people aren't being *difficult*—they are having *difficulty*. And maybe the one having the most difficulty was me.

Standing there with my hand stuck out, reeling from her anger and the sharp shrapnel lodged in the soft places, I saw only two options, two ways diverging in one darkening wood: the barrier way or the broken way.

We all have to choose. You can throw up a barrier to vainly keep the hurt out. Or you can break down your barriers, break right open, and let love with all its pain in. Either retreat behind useless, self-protecting barriers—or vulnerably lay the heart out there to be broken. Either slam up angry barriers with bricks of escapism, defensiveness, apathy, or distraction—or pick up your cross and choose the humility of vulnerability to break down all barriers and let someone in. And honestly, the loneliness of self-protecting barriers can feel like it will kill you—and the heart-breaking risk of intimacy and vulnerability can feel like it will kill you too.

I'd looked over at my daughter standing there in the trees and realized for all the supposed effectiveness of self-protective barriers, there isn't a barrier in the world that can block out pain. There isn't a wall you can build that protects you from pain. Addiction, escapism, materialism, anger, indifference—none of these can stop pain—and each one creates a pain all of their own. *There is no way to avoid pain. There is no way to avoid brokenness. There is absolutely no way but a broken way.*

Barriers that falsely advertise self-protection are guaranteed ways of self-imprisonment. Barriers that supposedly will protect your heart so it won't break are guaranteed to break your heart anyway.

Yet being brave enough to lay your heart out there to be broken, to be rejected in a thousand little ways, this may hurt like a kind of hell—but it will be holy. The only way in the whole universe to find connection . . . is to let your heart be broken. Love only comes to those brave enough to risk being brokenhearted.

"I already had one hand sticking out like a fool. So why not fling the other one out as well? So I did. I flung it open."

I wanted to be vulnerable and welcome it because I remembered that to thrive is to surrender to a kind of openness. I wanted to surrender control and trust One who is in control, even if I'd be taken beyond my control—even beyond what I felt I could bear. Maybe I thought it'd hurt more, but this strangely didn't hurt so much. Because in the moment, I wasn't afraid of her brokenness or mine or any brokenness between us, and all I could feel was a deepening intimacy. Her anger was like a kindness. A kind of plea for wholeness. A painful grace. She and I, we were taking this broken way and finding the depths of each other.

I thought in that moment, *This is what it means to be loved enough to be real, what it means to be connected and attached. This is what it means to be essentially alive, surrendered unshielded to the unknown because you know there is a deeper Love and He is knowable.*

She was staring me down, and I was hurting like Hades, but I said it like I was truly half unafraid. "Tell me more. Tell me how to make a safe place for a heart?"

Don't we all have to unlearn fear before we can truly learn to love?

Standing there in the woods where acorns have broken into

oaks, where seeds have broken into wheat, your scorched soul can feel it: you were made to grow into something more, but that only happens if you will be brave enough to break. Instead of giving someone a piece of your mind—it's far better to give them pieces of your heart.

So I tell Mei how the girl lashed at me and I listened and leaned into the passion of a suffering love. Listened to how she thought I'd been a heel, a lemon of a human being. How I seemed to have this harming coping mechanism of wanting to self-preserve instead of vulnerably serve. How she felt I hadn't given her a whole lot of courage, but more of a complex, and how I'd messed up her life because I was messed up. And I nodded right into that driving fury.

"You did?" Mei leans in.

I nod. Never become a container for anger. Anger is the only toxin that destroys what it's carried in. Somehow I found the good sense to remember it's when we defend our hearts and are deaf to the cries of other hearts . . . that the world becomes absurd—*surdus* in Latin, which means "deaf." The absurdity of hurt only changes when we stop being deaf and begin to *listen* to each other's hearts. *Audire* in Latin: "obedient." The way to a God-obedient life is to sincerely listen.

If we want to genuinely practice our faith, don't we need to genuinely listen? How would the world change if we all became masters in the art of hearing heartbeats? God's and His people's.

A leaf had fallen soundlessly between her and me. The dogs had barked off toward the road. Then everything had gone quiet. In the space between God and earth, Jesus became all ear. When we become all ear, this changes the sound of the world. I had stood there memorizing the outline of her face.

The kid had done it. She'd whipped around and given me the gift of baring where I broke her heart, and she let me hear its howling beat. Had she ever been more beautiful? Had I ever loved her more?

"I told her—I told her she was brave. For breaking open and giving me her pain. Trusting me enough to hold the shards of her heart." Beauty is not in your formidableness, but your fragility.

My quiet, deep-thinking daughter. I could have reached out and cupped the kid's brave face in my hands to assure her that beauty doesn't exist apart from fragility. Humanity's particular beauty is only *possible* because of its brave fragility. Look to your vulnerable God.

"So we stood in the woods and bled a bit." And it didn't matter that I knew how to get to the road because the only way I wanted now was a broken one.

"So, you got crucified?" Mei asks me point-blank.

"Basically—yeah." I swallow down the last of the tea gone cold but I'm warmed right through.

Mei says it slow: "Sometimes—some things have to break all apart so better things can be built."

I nod. *Never be afraid of broken things.* It's the beginning of better things. The best yields always start as broken fields.

"She told you," Mei says. "She gave you the gift of knowing where things are broken—which is the gift of knowing where to begin."

When you don't know where to begin and you're at the end of yourself, you get to be where all of God begins. What you always need most is *need*.

I sit with my cup right empty and this is all ending up feeling deeply fulfilling. *The way to feel the relief of a resurrection is to enter into the suffering of the Crucified.*

OUR MOST

MEANINGFUL PURPOSE

CAN BE FOUND

EXACTLY IN OUR MOST

PAINFUL BROKENNESS.

I'd once stood in another woods with an old man from church during a church cookout, and this old family friend turned to me under a drooping pine tree and said, "You took that dare to count all the ways He loves you, and it changed you, there's no denying that. It did." I'd nodded, agreeing.

The old guy had looked over at me. "It's true. You know you've been wooed by God a thousand times. But I'm asking you—no, I'm telling you: *dare to woo God*. Do you know how to do *that*?" He'd turned and walked ahead to his waiting wife.

I had experienced the wooing of God a thousand times—countless, endless times thanked Him for loving me. Like C. S. Lewis had written, "He can only woo."[1] I'd been Hosea's wife, Gomer and I'd been like Israel and I'd experienced what John Piper says of God's response to His people:

> *The first thing* he does is woo us tenderly: Verse 14: "Behold, I will allure her and bring her into the wilderness and speak tenderly to her." We are all guilty of harlotry. We have loved other lovers more than God . . . We, like Gomer, were enslaved to a paramour, the world, pleasure, ambition. But God has not cast us off. He promises to take us into the wilderness. He wants to be alone with us. Why? So that he can speak tenderly to us. Literally, the Hebrew says, so that he can speak "to her heart." And when he speaks, he will allure you. He will entice you and woo you. He will say what a lover says to his lady when they walk away from the party into the garden. God wants to talk that way with you. Go with him into the wilderness and listen with your heart. Do not think you are too ugly or too rotten. He knows that his wife is a harlot. That's the meaning of mercy: God is wooing a wife of harlotry.[2]

How many woods, how many wildernesses, had I found myself in? Had I known: God takes us into wildernesses not to abandon us—but to be alone with us? Wildernesses are not where God takes us to hurt us—but where He speaks to our hearts. Wildernesses can be safe because we are always safe when we are always with Him. Wildernesses can be where God woos. God had wooed me—a wife of harlotry. I have cried in deserts, been revived by the caress of His grace.

But was that even possible? To woo God? I didn't know if we could do that, or if I even had language for that. But take your one life and make wooing God your one aim, and how could that not woo you into the realest, most abundant living?

After the church cookout, I had come out at the edge of the woods and stood there, one hand propping up a thin ironwood tree, or it propping up me. And His Word can come through the trees like wind. "I was hungry and you fed me, I was thirsty and you gave me a drink, I was homeless and you gave me a room, I was shivering and you gave me clothes, I was sick and you stopped to visit, I was in prison and you came to me . . . I'm telling the solemn truth: Whenever you did one of these things to someone overlooked or ignored, that was me—you did it to me."[3]

The only way to love God . . . is to give to people. Love for Him has to turn into giving, or it was never love.

The only way to love God . . . is to give to people.

The only way to serve God . . . is to serve people.

The only way to woo God . . . is to care for the wounds of people.

The only way to woo God . . . is to let Him care for your wounds and give Him your brokenhearted need.

I could hear the old hymn coming up through the woods:

"All the fitness He requireth is to feel your need of Him . . . He is able, He is able; He is willing; doubt no more."[4]

Doubt no more—because He first embraces our heart wounds with His wooing; we are given effective strength and sufficient affection to woo Him back by reaching out and touching the wounds of the world with our own.

Doubt no more—because those who woo Jesus by living given—caress the face of Christ.

Maybe the only way to care for your wounds is to woo God. And you woo God by pressing your broken wounds into His, and finding that in Him, Him in you, you're touching the broken wounds of all the other wounded and entering the joy of Him—intimate communion, *koinonia*, with Him.

I carry my empty teacup into the kitchen, to the edge of the sink. I can see from the sink, through the open doorway to my room, the wall behind my desk. There's hanging this framed painting titled "Hands of Proof," a vivid depiction of Jesus' hand taking the hand of doubting Thomas and directing Thomas's hand to touch the bloody nail wound in Jesus' other open hand.

I hadn't noticed it before—but everything in the painting is a movement of Jesus. He moves Thomas's hand. He presses Thomas's doubt wounds into His own open wound. He offers His open wounds as the only home for ours. All healing is a movement of Christ—*He's doing it all.*

The dare to woo Jesus is a dare to press our wounds up to His broken heart and into the wounds of the world. And my dare to woo Jesus was a dare to press my wounds into that broken heart and into one girl's who went for a walk with me through the woods.

I could have *koinonia* here. I could have communion with Christ, I could share in the sufferings of Christ, not only by caring for her in her suffering, but also by coming to Christ with my own. We could woo God by caring for *all the wounds . . .* and Christ in us can heal them all. It's all wholly Him, His broken way. The brave baring of all the broken in their brokenness can offer the miracle of communion. *Never be afraid of being a broken thing.*

There's a chip in the handle of this teacup. I feel like I'm seeing everything for the first time.

He's inviting me to heal, but also to see my most meaningful calling: to be His healing to the hurting. My own brokenness, driving me into Christ's, is exactly where I can touch the brokenhearted. Our most meaningful purpose can be found exactly in our most painful brokenness. I'm not sure I'd known: *we can be brokers of healing exactly where we have known the most brokenness.*

Why have we swallowed the lie that we can only help if we're perfect? The cosmic truth sealed in the wounds of the broken God is that the greatest brokers of abundance know an unspoken broken. Wrapping my hands around the empty, cracked mug feels like this strange comfort. *It's all going to be okay.* What makes us feel the most disqualified for the abundant life is actually what makes us the most qualified. It's the broken and the limping, the wounded and the scarred, the stragglers and the strugglers, who may know best where to run with wounds. It's only the broken who know where the cracks are and how our broken wounds can be the very thin places that reveal God . . . and allow us to feel His safe holding hand.

Those who've known an unspoken broken can speak the most real healing.

Stay weak and dependent. This is how you stay strong in God. I don't bother mentioning it to Mei that day, because I really don't know how to bring it up—but the morning after the detour in the woods, the girl finds me at the stove with an empty pot in hand and she lays her head on my shoulder and whispers, "Mama? Yesterday? When you listened . . . I felt loved. When you owned things . . . I didn't feel so alone. Just—when you let my heart say everything—and you weren't afraid? . . . I felt close."

And I'd closed my eyes and let it come. Reached out to touch her cheek right there on my shoulder.

Maybe—safety is where the brokenness of two hearts meet.

Maybe there are these "'patches of Godlight' in the woods of our experience," like C. S. Lewis wrote.[5]

And maybe there can be a thousand ways out of the wilderness of our wounds, out of our woods, when there's this choosing the way to woo God.

Seventeen

How to Find the Heroes in a Suffering World

> *By compassion we make others' misery our own,*
> *and so, by relieving them, we relieve ourselves also.*
> THOMAS BROWNE

More than anything, you don't want to feel all alone in your unspoken broken. More than anything, all you've ever wanted is someone to hold you and say all your unspoken broken makes no difference—you are still held. The wounds that never heal are always the ones mourned alone. And you can tell yourself you're ready for God to heal it or use it however He wills, but that doesn't stop this quiet questioning of what it could mean or how it may feel. But you can go ahead and strap into a plane heading east, leaving the safety and comfort of home, because you're doing whatever it takes to move higher up and deeper into trusting God, what it takes to be in a different place by your next birthday, and one ten years from now.

Sometimes you don't know how wounded you are until you step out of your familiar ruts. Until you've slowed down, until you press your back up against the steadying strength of an oak tree on a humid Thursday out in some far-flung place and you look up into those tree limbs and realize half that tree is underground, and you can only see the half rooted in the light. That's when you can feel the wounded parts of you, the underground parts of you, how they'll do whatever it takes to keep reaching for the light.

How do you break yourself open so you're a safe place for broken hearts—and find the safe comfort that you long for, because you'll never be left alone?

A breeze rustles through a stand of oaks at the edge of the field like they already know. I'm standing under the shade in a field in Israel, where God Himself walked this beaten sod because maybe when you're trying to figure out how to walk the broken way—you go walk a mile or two where Jesus walked. You can see the goats and the sheep coming down the hillside, their fleece clotted with dead grass and fine dirt. The whole lot of them can't stop bleating, the whole flock oblivious to the howl of humanity.

The old and weathered man who drove us out to this field in the wilderness picks up the rod lying there across the roots of the tree, and says: "A shepherd is *only* about compassion and comfort."

I lean in. The sheep and goats linger in the rounding cool of the tree's limbs. Noonday heat runs in these silent, sticky rivulets down the hollow of my back. All hope of another breeze seems dead under this smother of blazing sun. That inked cross on my wrist is a sweat smudge, bleeding into pores.

"Seven ways, you hear me? You listening?" The bent farmer leans in to show us. "Seven ways a shepherd uses his staff to show his sheep compassion." He sticks the rod into the ground. Sun slides down its length and it seems to light like a candle. He leans it away from his body, making this V, and he waves for the sheep to come through between his bulk and the leaning rod. He shows us how he lays the rod out to guard the sheep, and then how it can become an extension of his arm.

"No matter what—always compassion, always love, see?" He nods, holding the rod out like a beckoning, like he's trying to invite us to see. The rod of God only moves to comfort and the ways of God are only compassion.

Wasn't this it, what I was looking for in the woods, what I couldn't see for the trees? The way to be a safe place for the brokenhearted is to let your heart always be a place of compassion.

"You've heard that a shepherd will break a sheep's leg if it wanders from the flock?" the man asks us, rod in his hand, rooted tree at his back. "You've heard this? Break its leg to keep it from breaking away from the flock?" He shakes his head, disgusted.

It's been preached from countless pulpits, how supposedly in ancient times, if a sheep kept darting off and getting miserably lost, the shepherd would resort to breaking its legs so it could no longer run off to danger. Then, after the breaking, the shepherd would nurse the broken sheep back to health so it would remain by the shepherd's side the rest of its limping life.

The air isn't merely hot out here; it's suffocating. Like standing at the edge of hell, the enemy himself exhaling sulfurous lies right into your dripping face. But little cups of dappled light have tipped out of the leaves of the tree, spilling across the backs of the sheep drifting in under a hillside oak tree.

"Look." He points his rod toward the flock slowly congregating. "A shepherd would never, ever break a sheep's bones. How would that be compassionate? How would that be merciful? Listen—this is what a shepherd does."

And he explains that a shepherd may put a "brake" on a sheep's leg—a weight to temporarily stop a stiff-necked sheep from running astray. And once the sheep is close, once the sheep learns its own name, once the sheep learns the voice of the shepherd and the way he calls her—that sheep learns not to be afraid, to never be afraid. She trusts the ways of the shepherd. The sheep turn and wander a path straight up the side of the hill. And something in me opens, like a returning to the fold. All those broken ways that seemed like dead ends? The ways that twisted and felt like betrayals? All the ways I felt abandoned when my sister's skull was crushed and broken in front of me and the years of emotional neglect and locked psych wards eroded away the only home I'd known, when my parents' divorce tore the last crumbling brick out and everything left to cling to imploded? When I'd felt the anxiety of Hope inevitably sliding into my same escapist trap there at the window overlooking wheat and forgot for a moment how to breathe, the weight I'd felt that morning I woke on my birthday? When I'd turned around in the woods thinking I knew the "right" way that wasn't? Hadn't all of this been forging a kind of better, broken way?

What if all the years, all the wandering and wounded ways, what if it all found fully sufficient grace just there: sometimes what we think may break us is but a brake to save us. Sometimes what we feel weighing us down is the way He draws us closer. Sometimes what we believe is keeping us from more is a way to keep us close enough to know more of who we are: *beloved.* What feels like too much can give you more of God. And you can always have as much of God as you want. You can always have an abundance of God if that's what you want. And the things that feel like breaking things can be things that brake you from pulling away from God—things that pull you closer.

Out of nowhere, this exhale of a breeze comes, like an

invisible ocean of relief. What do you say when wounds you didn't know you even had are touched with a compassion you didn't know existed?

Maybe it's the compassion of God that uses the unexpected to brake me so the unholy doesn't break me. What's slowing me down and braking me could be a gift that's keeping me from breaking into a bad brokenness.

"Always remember this . . . always compassion, always love."

The leaves rise. The grey-haired man speaks with this whispered, gravelly kindness, lifts his rod toward the lingering sheep. "There is a Shepherd who let Himself be broken *so the sheep don't ever have to be broken.*"

And it's like one of those cups of light up in the tree's dappled shade had tipped and the realization is like an ointment for wounds: Jesus' compassionate, perfect heart never demands the self-mutilation, self-condemnation, or self-emancipation of imperfect hearts. Jesus' compassion never holds us to a standard of perfection, but always holds us in His arms of grace. I think—for years I'd covertly actually been one of those Baal worshipers who cut themselves until their blood flowed for all the idols that relentlessly demanded more and more.[1] I think—there had been years of mornings of breaking myself on the altars of a thousand merciless idols, a thousand cruel Baals—the Baal of success, of perfection, of Pinterest, of acceptance, validation, affirmation. How many of us don't even know that we're striving Baal cutters, performing all the dance steps around some altar of a god of acceptance, so that if we give enough of ourselves, we earn some rain of approval?

I hadn't known it like this: You know you've got an idol to break whenever you feel broken by performance. You know you have a Baal idol that needs to be cut and broken down whenever you want to cut and break yourself down. Whenever you slash and break yourself, you have an idol that needs to be slashed and broken down.

Because isn't that what every idol ultimately wants: to make you perform like mad and break yourself for it and drive you right into the unforgiving ground? Every idol wants you to be cut and broken open for it.

There is a Shepherd who let Himself be broken so the sheep don't ever have to be broken. He let His blood run so you can stop running. The sheep and the goats are this stilled ring of quiet around the oak tree in the corner of the field.

That cross inked on my wrist has left a mirror image on my leg. My body being shaped cruciform. All these things inside of me taking shape: the only way to break the idols in your life is to accept what Jesus gives you freely that every other god demands but that you can never achieve. Jesus comes to *give* you freely through His passion what every other god forces you to try to *get* through performance.

I trace the little blurred cross on my leg. How can I not ache with a grateful love for a compassion like this? And how could His compassion for me not compel me to give His compassion to the aching?

The sheep and the goats lap from the river running gold in the slanted light and it's a fresh revelation I'm drinking in: compassion isn't saccharine sentimentality; it's key to humanity's survival. Compassion heals what condemnation never could. I lap it up—what I'm parched for, what the world's parched for: Jesus is drawn to the broken with a deep compassion. Jesus is drawn to *my* deep broken with a deep compassion.

Safety is found where the brokenness of two hearts meet. The relief of it runs down into the wounds of me.

The breeze picks up through all the rooted limbs of the leaning oak trees. And it feels a bit divine.

When I return home after a handful of days walking the ways and the fields where Jesus walked, I step in the back door to a load of wet laundry dumped right in front of the back door, a bag of oozing trash ripped apart by a zealous puppy, and a rotting squash leaking all over the bottom of this bowl on the kitchen counter. A swarm of fruit flies circle like tiny vultures and I want to, very nicely, break someone's neck.

Compassionately, of course.

I don't feel one dripping iota of compassion for the laundry dumper. I have this undeniable, embarrassing urge to give the garbage-rooting puppy a soccer-sized kick out the back door. And I don't even try to stifle this raging rant at the kids for the fruit flies.

When I get my hands really flailing, I can see the cross I've inked right there on the wrist and I suddenly think how theology is an exercise in futility unless it's exercised under our roofs, unless it's exercised with our hands and our feet. How in God's holy name can I go from knowing fully God's unspeakable compassion, standing there under an oak tree with a flock of sheep, to having a full-blown raging reaction under my own roof with a mess of my own?

The young oak trees right outside our front window, they grow through summer days, age with these rings of light all around the trunk. How do you accumulate light, age with rings of light around your heart? You wouldn't guess I cared a flying

fig that Spurgeon said, "If you would sum up the whole character of Christ in reference to ourselves, it might be gathered into
this one sentence, 'He was moved with compassion.'"[2]

Moved with compassion?

Does that mean compassion isn't an occasional stance only
when we are moved, but a mark of character, the entire posture of how we can move through our lives? What if the whole
revolving earth wasn't fueled by ambition, but was moved with
compassion?

"To be moved with compassion"—that phrase, it's spoken
of in Scripture only in regard to Christ and our Father, and it's
splanchnizomai in the Greek—and it's what we'd call guts.

When Christ was moved with compassion, it's like He got
kicked in the gut.

When Christ's people feel compassion like Christ did, and
they feel the strike to the stomach—they feel the pain in the
deepest places, and they hurt and they bend over and they
reach down and they reach out and their lives become cruciform, shaped into the cross of Christ.

Compassion isn't merely a vague sense—but a feeling so
strong that it causes you to bend. It shapes your body, your life,
into a response.

Compassion is the radical cross-shaping of a life.

Sometimes I can actually feel that cross on my wrist: live the
posture of Christ, stretched out there on a tree. Hands broken
wide open to embrace the Christ in everyone, embrace the grace
in everything. Hands broken wide open to receive the gifts in
everything and give those gifts to everyone.

Everything broken open. Brokenhearted openness.
Brokenhearted vulnerability. Brokenhearted intimacy.

Cruciform.

How else can you make Christ's presence known apart from cruciform compassion? What if the only way to move forward in any situation is to always be moved with compassion?

It's relatively easy to pontificate on how to live the gospel; it's infinitely harder to incarnate the gospel in your life. I want to shake my own hard heart awake.

If Jesus felt compassion more than any other feeling, can we learn?

The word means "together," *com*, and "to suffer," *pati*. Compassion is about co-passion, about co-suffering. You only have compassion where you are willing to co-suffer.

So, some kid had nothing to wear and the clock was cracking its relentless hands across his back and he dumped out the wet laundry from the dryer before its time, because he and his just washed jeans were running out of time. But clearly, the dog and the squash offender have no credible defense.

Exactly. Exactly how many times have I had no credible defense and a Shepherd had compassion on me, co-suffered with me, suffered alone for me?

The two youngest kids, Kai and Shalom, are on their knees in the mudroom picking up the soggy garbage. The tallest kid's standing there in the kitchen with his hands stuffed in his pockets, telling me he really doesn't have time to clean up the puddling rot on the counter.

Of course, son—my words drip with sarcasm—there's got to be someone else whose life isn't nearly as pressing who can mop up the stench you've let puddle across where we prepare the food.

Why is condemnation so quick in our veins and compassion so sluggishly slow? Whenever faith loses its compassion, its co-suffering—it co-hosts demons. I could weep. Scraping the squash gunk that has dried on the stove and I know I'm muttering it too loud: "Everybody's got time to change the world, but no one's got time to help Mom clean up the kitchen."[3]

I turn, look steadily into the eyes of my boy. And louder than the fury in my head is the bleating of those sheep when they came down that hillside. "He was moved with compassion."[4]

Suddenly, the six-foot-one boy looks small to me, broken to me. People don't have to be good to deserve our compassion; it's our compassion that serves good to all people.

I rinse out the stinking cloth over the sink. Why do I keep forgetting? Life isn't overwhelming when you simply understand how to serve in this minute.

Why in the blazes is compassion-that-serves so bloody hard? Why is dying so hard?

It's one thing to have enough compassion when you're standing in an oak tree's island of shaded stillness watching the quietness of sheep, listening to the fractures of your heart re-member itself—it's another thing to incarnate it. Anyone can have enough compassion to write a check for the needy, but who has compassion for the kid who makes life hard?

Compassion can feel like the right thing when it involves a donation. But when there's been a violation of your rights? Compassion can feel like degradation.

No one has to holler it too loud to me—sometimes the Spirit speaks the clearest in the quiet. He's a wind and I'm a bell, rung with conviction. Everyone wants to change the world, but who wants to change the laundry over? Everyone's passionate about changing the world, but who's changing themselves to find compassion in their own world?

God help me. Literally. *God. Help. Me.*

When all else fails, those three words never fail. God. Help.

Me. The song of the poor in spirit. He breaks in before I get to the refrain. He comes.

Only communion in the presence of the God of compassion can make anyone compassionate.

"You want me to light some candles, Mama?" Hope's standing there in the mess. The long lit candle she's got in her hand, it looks like a staff. She lights the candle at the sink. She looks like she's come looking for me.

Why do we want to be publicly known in far-flung places for our great compassion instead of knowing a great compassion in the places we live? You can find yourself under your own roof, looking at your own people, and your own mess of unspoken broken, and there it is like a light:

> There's more abundance
> in daily giving your presence to one
> than daily diligence for the furtherance of hundreds.

It is more like Christ to go after the one than to go after the applause of the ninety-nine. There is more compassion in the giving of yourself in hidden, dying ways to the unworthy than there is in giving expensive things in noticed ways to the applauding.

The dishcloth's like a hot pleading in my hand, scrubbing down the front of the stove. C'mon, heart—come break yourself and give yourself and die to self, one thousand little deaths, and co-suffer: com-passion.

Compassion isn't a trite feeling of the heart as much as it's a willing breaking open of the heart; com-passion isn't easy, because co-suffering isn't easy. And compassion is always dying to bits of you because there is no other way for there to be resurrection.

EVIL CAN BE THE CAUSE

OF ALL KINDS OF SUFFERING,

BUT ALL SUFFERING

DOES NOT HAVE TO BE EVIL.

Was that it—compassion asks you to suffer with fools? Compassion asks you to suffer with the foolishness of impossible systems and unfair oppression, suffer with the foolishness of miserable policies and a myriad of complicated people. Hadn't a Shepherd suffered with my foolishness—for my foolishness? Maybe if your faith doesn't co-suffer with people, it isn't faith; it's cowardice.

I should have seen that, standing there under that stretched-out oak tree, watching the sheep, and thinking of a broken Shepherd: *compassion will always hurt.* Compassion is a crawling in under the skin of someone else and connecting to their heart like it's yours. Your heart breaks into theirs and your way is bound to theirs and don't tell me that's not profoundly terrifying. But it's profoundly purifying and sanctifying and God-glorifying and soul-unifying—and ultimately, life-satisfying. It's precisely through this communion of compassion that a soul finds the connectedness it seeks. Yes, it will hurt, but it will heal. Yes, you must grow weak enough to love the world, and yet strong enough to let Christ carry your cross and all the willing world's or you will be crushed by all of it. And yes, compassion says there will only be abundance for me when there is abundance for you, so I will be bread broken and given to you so we both can taste the communion of abundance.

I'm standing there scrubbing down the front of the stove, tasting the holy burn of an epiphany, there in the back of my throat, when my phone vibrates. Malakai grabs it, hands it to me.

It's blinking up and bleeding right there across the screen: "It's in the bones. Tamara's cancer—it's now in her bones."

I lean against the counter. Where's a busted staff to lean on when you need it? *Where in the name of a good God is the Shepherd?*

"It's Mrs. Kindsley . . ." The words sort of fall out of a crack in my heart.

"Her cancer's back?" Malakai leans in to read my eyes.

There are voids of light in the canopy of leaves out in that young oak tree by the road, shafts of light where leaves left too soon. I hold my reeking cloth, stopped. By God, why can't we get all this monstrous cancer to stop?

First, her breast. Then her lymph nodes, then her lungs. Now it's in her bones. First Elizabeth. Then Kara. Now Tamara. Tamara's forty-four. With two little kids at home and their dad long gone. It's staggering how quick the mess in the kitchen and one soggy squash can evaporate into insignificance in the grand cosmic scheme of things.

"Mama?" Shalom steps over strewn garbage to throw her arms around me. She presses into me like she's holding on for dear life. Her whole little life she's played on the front lawn of the chapel after Sunday service with Tamara's kids. She looks up at me. Her hair's falling into her face and I brush it back so I can see her eyes. And she whispers it to me like all of earth could quake heaven with that one word:

"Why?"

Why? Why has Mrs. Kindsley's cancer spread to her begging bones, why does she have to tell her Caleb and Emma that the chemo is not working at eating up the monstrous cancer? Why do two little kids have to go to bed wondering what will happen if their mama dies?

And I look right into her and nod slow. Oh, child. I know that howl of why. "Relent, Lord! How long will it be? Have compassion on your servants."[5] Have compassion on us who are but dust, who are weary and desperate to pry open the door in the universe and find You taking all our wrong and making it right.

The broken way begins with this lost art of lament and until we authentically lament to God, we'll never feel authentically loved by God.

Lament's not a meaningless rage, but a rage that finds meaning in His outrageous love. Lament is an outrage . . . that still trusts in God's good outcome. Lament's this articulation of the ache at God's abandonment, then an acquiescence to His ache, and finally an abandonment to His will. Go ahead, child. Lament carries brokenness in its hands straight into the heart of God and asks for His arms. In the midst of suffering, no one needs clarifying arguments as much as they need to feel arms close. So He gives an experience of Himself instead of mere explanations, because He knows explanations can be cold comfort and His arms are warm.

What warms us is the wounded, weeping God who doesn't write any answers in stars but writes His ardent love for us with His wounds. Right into our wounds.

"Maybe the love gets in easier right where the heart's broke open?"

Malakai drops the garbage bag, leans into Shalom, and whispers, "You want to know why, Shalom?"

Shalom turns to him, her eyes glistening liquid, and he puts his arm around her shoulder. "This is what I think." He pulls Shalom closer to him, leans his forehead into hers, says it slow: "This is how I always think about it: pain is like a pack of wolves attacking sheep, and it's pain that always brings out the heroes."

I smile—I never knew this moved in the boy. I reach out, touch his cheek. He buries himself in my shoulder. Hard things can bring out good things. *We don't have to be afraid.* There's a Shepherd whose compassion, whose co-suffering, works in us to make even the broken into co-heroes with Him. I hold my kids tight in a mess of garbage and who knows what to say in the face of wolves in the woods and nightmares lurking? Do you tell them we don't need answers to why God allows evil as much as how to hold on to the goodness of God amidst unanswered questions? Do you say evil and suffering do not need to be explained as much as to be absorbed? *Love is a roof.* The focus of God's people is not to create explanations for suffering, but to create communities around suffering, co-suffering communities to absorb suffering and see it transform into cruciform grace. This will cost us. This will remake us into the image of Christ.

Do you tell them how it's taking decades of wrestling with God to know this: evil can be the cause of all kinds of suffering, but all suffering does not have to be evil?

They say our universe is made of atoms, but it is made of suffering. Because it is made of love. I want to tell them this: the world was made out of love and it was made for love, which means the world is the essence of vulnerability and fragility and suffering.

I want to sear them with this, brand myself with this, the woman with chronic soul amnesia, who tries to divorce suffering at every turn, who tries to escape it at first sight. Why do I want to escape love? *Evil can be the cause of all kinds of suffering, but all suffering does not have to be evil. To love is to suffer.* Instead of flexing His muscle, He surrendered His muscle to the nail. Instead of leveraging His position, He leveraged Himself out on a cross. He made sacrifice His default position. Instead of stonewalling people with His authoritative power, He laid down His authority, lay down in a tomb, lay in a suffering death till the stone was rolled away. The broken way made this cosmos, proving that the greatest power in the universe is the suffering of a brokenhearted love. The greatest power in the universe is the power of the broken way.

For crying out loud, woman. Take that broken way.

Do I whisper it in their ears, right now? Ultimately evil is simply a turning away from good; evil is ultimately turning away from God.

And by God, the evil is in us, in me. One mess in my kitchen can swing this head right around and away from the Shepherd and the faces of these kids. I don't want to waste it like this, pointing at evil and breaking my gaze from Him. How easily I can become a sliver of the evil instead of a gift.

Evil is always a function of distractions, a turning away from God. *Make the ever-present Christ present . . . by being present.*

Evil is to experience suffering without meaning, without God. Perhaps the "problem of evil" is more importantly a problem of not seeing meaning, a problem of not seeing God. Hopelessness is what flings one into the presence of evil.

In the trees outside the window, time's swallowing the light. A breeze breaks through the reaching branches with a defiant rumor of eternity.

This is a whisper that could break the chains around a thousand reaching hands: evil is only that which breaks us away from God. But evil is broken when you don't let brokenness break you away from God.

The light out in the oak trees and that lone maple, it's breaking up all the shadows. Leaves cling to the limbs. There are leaves that look entwined—like one.

The answer to the problem of evil is everything that lets us keep loving God—even in the face of evil.

"Mama—" Kai's voice feels more like an answer than a question. How had I never seen that there are a thousand, countless answers to the problem of evil, countless graces that keep us loving God? "Mama, what's going to happen now for

Mrs. Kindsley?" His eyes are large, searching mine. He's in the same Sunday school class as Tamara's daughter. He's seen the ravages of chemo, the stinging ooze of the mouth sores, the hell of the pain. He's looking for some steadying staff. The candle Hope lit by the sink, its flame is burning straight and sure.

"For the LORD *has comforted his people and will have compassion on his afflicted."*[6]

"Look—" I lay my hand on Kai's neck, pull him in nearer. He's warm with the light moving through the trees, through the window, across the floor. "What's going to happen now for Mrs. Kindsley? Exactly what you said."

There will be heroes. There will be heroes who keep their eyes on the Shepherd, who let the Shepherd and His compassion live in them. That's how He makes real heroes. It's Jesus who fills us up with this light of compassion, with the compassion He's shown us, and we can become heroes, co-sufferers. The heroes are the ones who carry their broken cups of light into the world to leak His healing light. We will bring her His grace, a listening ear, a meal, an invitation to our table, a bunch of wildflowers; we will give her the gift of presence. We will make Christ present, we will be the GIFT, and we will give her cup upon cup of light.

When you give your broken heart as a cup of His light, all the broken fills with His light.

The candle at the sink flickers, cupping flame, and I want to finally embrace what I keep forgetting: it's when we truly pay attention to people that we get to co-suffer with people. Paying attention is one of the purest forms of compassion. *Had that Shepherd's eyes ever left attending to His own?*

It's only the suffering that is not shared that leads to a singular kind of insanity.

Suffering need not be a barrier to communion. In fact, it can be a door into its warming light.

Kai laces his fingers through mine, squeezes tight—and I pull him close, kiss his forehead, press my plea into his.

The question of evil does not need a solution as much as it needs compassion. Because *compassion is the solution.* Suffering is not a problem that needs a *solution* as much as it's an experience that needs *compassion.*

Because the universe rings with just this one song: "Even if a mother might not have compassion on her son, I will never forget you, I will leave the ninety-nine for you, I will suffer for you. Though you feel helplessly lost, impossibly wounded, hopelessly despairing, I will always be moved with compassion for you.

"My name is Compassion[7] and I will not break you, but I will break Myself for you. I am the compassionate Shepherd calling a thousand heroes to carry the light of My compassion to the broken. I will come across a thousand fields with an army of brokenhearted light-bearers for you. And you are never safer than when you feel Me redeeming your unspoken broken.

"And if you forget this? I will never forget and I will never forget you and this is what My unstoppable compassion does: *Behold, I have engraved you, you, on the palms of My hands.*"[8]

There is nothing to fear in the wilderness of suffering—it is the land where God woos. The crush of crisis is but a passage into communion with Christ.

I reach out to pick up a torn envelope from the dog's mess of garbage strewn across the floor. My name's written across it. Shalom whispers: "Look—your hand in the light right there like that. It looks like it's a cup of light."

The child's grinning like we've all been found.

When I wake the next morning, I read it in that Old Book, right there in Isaiah: ". . . still others will write on their hand, 'The LORD's.'"⁹ And I turn over my hand in sunlight. That fading inked cross there on my wrist. Marked. One of His. To feel His compassion and to carry His compassion, to co-suffer.

My name on His hand. His name on mine. *I am His and He is mine.*

Is that what I'm doing with this ridiculous experiment of penning a cross on my wrist? With just those two cross strokes, it's like I am writing my way and my name and my identity: Enough. There is enough. Abundantly enough.

I am enough, because I have enough of Him and He is always enough, and that is enough for anything. I am signing my name and my identity and being signed by the Cross One, the Risen One. I am shaping my life and letting my life be shaped, writing it down into me so it literally forms me: a passionate life is a sacrificial life. A life that wants to embrace Christ is a life that must embrace suffering. A life of giving is ultimately the most life-giving. And every single time I sign that cross on my wrist, I'm guaranteeing I can always find my sign from God, pointing the way forward—*given*. Broken and given into communion with Him and a thousand ways to reach right out and give it forward into the broken community of the world.

A signed and sealed sign that there isn't anything I can possibly do to make Him love me more. And in everything I am loved more than I can possibly imagine.

It's strange how an open hand cupping light looks like it's rooted to the sky.

Eighteen

Why You Don't Have to Be Afraid to Be Broken

Can they—these messy, dirty, poisoned wounds—
can they themselves cure us?

MARK BUCHANAN

The day I had first met Mei, she was holding twelve babies.

Not all at once, mind you. But she had their photos there on the phone in her back pocket and she held them out on that screen to me like she was showing me a ring, like she was showing me priceless things.

I'd leaned in.

"This is Ruby."

Small and wide-eyed. Shy, toothy smile. Silk-black sprout with this red bow on the top of her head.

All down the street, behind Mei, there's a bluing darkness catching in the trees.

And then she flicks up Zeke. Kate. Sarah. Twelve babies living in Mei's house in Beijing.

"Those are their English names," she tells me, scrolling through more photos. Chinese names: Yu Xin. Fei. Quan Ting.

"And they were—"

I can't say the word.

"Yeah, they were . . ." she nods slowly, throwing her dark braid over her shoulder, and speaking the word I can't say: "abandoned."

I'd put my bag down. Mei moved closer, hand holding her phone and their pictures so I can see them in the light.

Every one of them—babies with umbilical cords cut and then they themselves cut off. Reaching my hand out, the one with penned cross on the wrist, I take her phone.

"And . . . they were abandoned because?" I look up at Mei.

Mei looks down at the phone, down at my penned wrist.

"Broken hearts," she says it so quietly I have to lean in closer. "All of them—congenital heart defects. Parents can't pay the bills for the heart surgeries. So they wrap them up in blankets, with a bottle, maybe a note pinned to the edge of the blanket, and leave them outside of hospitals, in town squares, near police stations."

I'm leaning over this gallery of their photos, these brown searching eyes. Who holds the abandoned and forgotten? Everything in that moment's echoing Kierkegaard—"Who am I? How did I get into the world? Why was I not asked about it? And if I am compelled to be involved, where is the manager—I have something to say about this."[1]

Where is the manager? *I need to see Him.*

"They are abandoned . . ." Mei traces Ruby's face on her phone's screen, "because their hearts are broken." The streetlight's flitting like fireflies blinking bravely—relentlessly looking for that evasive something of home across the dark.

I look up at Mei. She nods slowly.

You can feel abandoned because your heart is too broken for somebody—and your heart can feel too broken . . . because you've been abandoned by somebody.

The streetlights blink on.

Maybe the light never stops coming for us, beckoning us. Carrying us home with our hidden shards. The cross on my wrist is catching bits of the light.

"How?" I'm pointing at this picture on her phone of all these babies with emblazoned scars right down the middle of their chests. "How do you do all this?"

Mei looks me steady in the eye.

"You just . . . can't be afraid of a broken heart."

I don't know how long I stood there staring at her, listening to the buzzing streetlights—this rush of an awakening to my life in my ears.

Month rolling into month, I try, and kind of fail, but try again, to stay present to Mei and her babies because she and her babies have stayed present with me. The gift of presence is easy when the road keeps rising to meet you. She's a lone warrior in a foreign land, dogged by numbing policies and tangled red tape, fighting to save one abandoned, heart-broken baby at a time. When you know someone who's slaying dragons, you want to offer them a safe place to rest. But maybe also I read something burning there in her eyes that night that I don't quite understand but know I need to.

Whenever she calls, I pick up. When she needs a reprieve from the battle for the abandoned and brokenhearted, Mei comes and we eat together and walk the fields and inhale and exhale under the wide open sky. The autumn woods with leaves falling seem heavy with the scent of surrender. That Mason jar of wheat sits on the windowsill. Twenty-five thousand five hundred fifty kernels—my life. We walk by it a hundred times.

I send a stitched quilt across the Pacific to her in Beijing and learn what to send babies with thin skin and dropping oxygen levels, longing to impart a love that began before Calvary and can slay all the dark. But one of the babies, Ruby, continues to fade, her fingers bluing like a bruised night sky. When a picture flashes up on my screen, for just one moment, I've got to turn, dam against the tsunami of panic. Ruby's purple lips look grape-stained. Her heart's being crushed.

Mei rushes Ruby to surgeons all across smog-choked Beijing. Half a globe away, I'm trying to re-member to breathe. The surgeons' collective shaking of heads rattles me thousands of miles away: *inoperable*. Mei grabs a scrap of paper and draws them a picture of a shunt. "Would you try this?" she asks, shoving it across a table at a surgeon. When he agrees, I can feel Mei's exhale undo things in my own knotted chest. In the body of Christ, how one person breathes affects the whole body.

All night I sit up with Mei, watching the slow arms of the clock while surgeons cut a baby open and try to patch her dying heart. The chance she'll roll out of that surgical theater alive? With a heart still pounding courage in her chest? "Twenty-five percent," the surgeon said.

Ruby's wheeled out alive.

Mei steps outside the hospital to breathe relief. A double rainbow rings the sky over her. She takes a picture and messages it to me. I cry and there's absolutely no shame in tears that water your praise or prayers. There are promises ringing the fellowship of the broken in shades that we only get to glimpse now and then.

And maybe because she knows hospitals, maybe that's why

I messaged her first? That seems logical, practical. But when things started to unravel a bit that Saturday morning in early January, maybe I really reached out to her first because, though I wouldn't have admitted it then, I remembered what I'd seen burning in her eyes that night.

After everything had broken and crumbled a bit, after the Farmer and I had hung on to each other, met with the doctor and nurses, after the whirlwind had left us with a bit of emotional debris, after he'd kissed my forehead softly and headed back to our children at home, I leave Mei a message:

> Too early. I'm sorry. Was in ER, now been admitted. Kai is sick—lost 20 pounds in 2 weeks, bruised half-moons under his eyes. Gaunt. Doctor says Type 1 diabetes, 4–6 insulin needles a day for the rest of his life. Just setting in that this isn't like a broken arm and in 6 weeks the cast comes off. Constant insulin awareness or death . . . Yeah, you can make your plans—but it's God's plans that happen. Maybe grieving over plans changed is part of the plan to change us.

A nurse rolls a cart of medications down the dim hallway. Faith is confidence in the kindness of God, no matter the confusion of circumstances. I turn, tap it out to Mei:

> Everybody's going to be fine, really, just need a minute to pull ourselves together here.

Sometimes, it's more than being afraid of any broken things—we're afraid to be a burden to anyone. Sometimes—we just can't bear the thought that our brokenness might break anyone else. Sometimes—it seems easier to bury our hurt than break anyone's heart.

I brush my cheeks with the back of my hand, exhale, pull my shoulders up, step back into the hospital room. A nurse is bent over Kai, showing him how to set an insulin needle to the right dose. Kai pulls up his shirt, aims the needle at his own skin, injects his belly with 21 units of insulin, dabs away the bit of blood. He looks over at me, grin half-cocked, questioning, and I wink back at his brave. After the boy falls asleep, I stand in the greying light of the window.

> I know you're still sleeping in Beijing—but I'm reading stuff I shouldn't be. Make me stop? Like: Type 1 diabetes, may reduce normal lifespan by 10–15 years. One in 20 younger people with Type 1 Diabetes will die in their sleep.
> All I can think: 10 less complete spins around the sun, 10 less birthday cakes, 10 less. I want him to have those 10 too. I want him to keep waking up. Just—heartbroken. We're going to be fine, really, we are. If I could just stop everything running down my face.

It was the slightest crack—but my broken heart was giving away.

I lay the phone down on the windowsill, lay my forehead against the cold windowpane.

It's like the Farmer said: it feels like we just joined a club. The club of the broken, this club with medicine bottles and needle marks and doctor appointments, hurting in hidden ways, beating back the grief and the grave. My throat burns. Maybe it's okay to not feel strong, to carry an unspoken broken. And . . . to speak it?

My phone flashes.

Hey, you. Just sitting with you here. It's okay. It's okay
to not be okay.

Let it come . . . Let it come. The letters all swim a bit on the
screen. Maybe you can't compare suffering, can't rank or minimize
suffering, but simply embrace it and all the others suffering too.
I type out:

Thanks for being a safe place to come with a mess of
broken.

Kai rolls over in the bed, the rails creak. A bed wheels down
the hall. And then she says:

You know what you just did—you just came and
gave your heart. You just laid out your broken heart,
without me asking for it.

I lean against the wall. *What?*

I think this is the first time since I've known you that
you've opened your heart. You came to me and
voluntarily shared.

I type back, my fingers pausing over the letters, trying to
decipher what my heart's pounding out:

You mean—are you saying you've always had to
commit a break and entry—to get into my heart?

The room's still. The fluorescent light hums over Kai's bed.

Yeah—something like that. But this time—you gave
yourself without being asked.

I'm shaking my head. *This* time? *This* time I gave? What
about all the other times? Hadn't I sacrificed myself, my time?
Hadn't I been giving to her, been willing to be inconvenienced
for her, emptied a bit of my bucket for her? This whole time,
hadn't I intentionally chosen to be broken and given?

I need to sit.

I read:

You just gave—your broken heart.

And the room begins to fall away all around me.

After everything I had given her—what Mei had really
wanted me to give her . . . was a bit of my own brokenness?

I think—I was always reluctant to share any of my own
brokenness with you because I didn't want to add to
your own life that was full to the point of breaking?
Didn't want to be a burden. Didn't want to cause—
more breaking.

Mei replies:

Yeah, I know. But you know—that is why I didn't think
we were real friends.

I've got to grab the green vinyl chair at the end of the bed,
sit down.

If I don't fully share my own brokenness . . . there's never full communion? Maybe—communion can only happen when not only our strong parts are broken and given, but when our broken parts are also given. Maybe communion happens not only when we're broken and given—but *when we give each other our brokenness.*

My heart's beating louder than anything else I can hear. I'm feeling along the edge of something I've never fully felt: Maybe what's given out of strength can show care through our willingness to give. But everything given out of our brokenness can show greater love through our willingness to *suffer.* Any healing communion that we can give will come not through our strength, but *through our brokenness.*

Kai's sleeping. The snow's falling. And something is falling like the gentlest grace on me.

Generosity does give birth to intimacy—but there's a far deeper intimacy when we're generous in sharing our brokenness. If you can be brave enough, vulnerable enough, humble enough, trust enough, and give the most broken shards of your heart to another believing broken heart . . . then is it your own broken shards that can best open up another heart?

In the stillness of a hospital room, I wonder if that isn't what I've been waiting so long to do, to . . . break open my own heart?

While there is deep wisdom in reserving our hearts with those who don't love through Christ's broken heart, there's even deeper wisdom in trusting enough to share our broken hearts with those who do. The more we seek Christ's broken heart in others, maybe the more we will find it, and the safer we'll find we are to share our own broken hearts with them.

The light's circling across the floor, around my feet, my hands, and this exhale comes like a quiet hush over the inner anxiety. There is no fellowship for brokenhearted believers while protecting others from our own brokenness—because we are the fellowship of the broken . . . and fellowship happens in the brokenness. *The miracle happens in the breaking.*

I trace that cross on my wrist slow, outline the beams. It's exactly the places of brokenness that let the need and power of the cross bleed through.

I hear you saying . . . And without allowing people to participate in our sufferings—there is never any intimate communion.

How had I tried to avoid suffering, mask my suffering, terminate all suffering instead of sharing it, letting others participate in my own, choosing to stand with others in theirs, stay with their suffering and break the heart open and let people into all of my own—so the suffering might be shaped into an intimacy that *transcends* and *transforms* the suffering? The heart has a far greater capacity for pain than can even be imagined—because it can love far greater than ever imagined.

There are needles on Kai's bedside stand. There's my reflection in the hospital window, hospital lights burning behind me. Sometimes you feel a bit like you're in a house on fire and there's a crowd outside trying to save you, trying to help you, trying to give you something to hold on to—but you've locked your door and you're burning alone in your fire. And you need at least one person to stop trying to save or rescue you, one person to ignore all the panic and alarms, and just come sit with you in your burn. In your burn all you need is to feel the heart of Christ burning for you. And you can feel the heart of Christ burning for you through broken hearts reaching toward you in your burn.

IT'S ALWAYS

THE VULNERABLE HEART

THAT BREAKS

BROKEN HEARTS FREE.

Everyone needs someone to be with them in the burn.

This can turn the flames into a holy blaze. Someone just choosing to be with you in your fire with a bit of theirs—can turn out to be better than anyone trying to extinguish your fire. Shared flames and shared burn scars can ignite hearts into a great fire that fights fire.

The fluorescent light over Kai's bed keeps humming, flickering.

If you can sit in your burn and brokenness and let it break down all your walls—so you can live into the givenness of even your brokenness—the crisis can bond you to Christ and other broken hearts.

The hospital room feels like a holy kind of beauty. Like a visitation.

With-ness breaks brokenness.

God with us. He names Himself that: *Immanuel.* God with us—because with-ness breaks brokenness. God's with us in the fire. Maybe—suffering doesn't have to torch life purpose, but can ultimately achieve the true purpose of life—intimacy. Where suffering is shared, communion is tasted. And maybe the fellowship of the broken—*koinonia* in the brokenness—begins to mitigate that suffering. Isn't that what I could now feel—with-ness breaking brokenness?

There's a cross bleeding into my thin skin, that's with me in my veins, in my cracked heart.

The sky outside the hospital window moves closer. There are stars out there that are larger than all the other stars. Those are the ones that are actually two stars attached, connected—rotating around each other, burning and breaking with so much gravitational pull there's no space for anything else. In the whole vastness of space, they're with each other in the breaking burn.

A chair scrapes somewhere down the hall. I can see headlights trailing down hospital side streets, down toward the church. Headlights catch in that surrendered cross suspended atop the steeple.

You may be called by Christ to be broken and given to the world, but you only become like Christ when you give your brokenness to the world. Everyone needs communion in their brokenness and Christ always comes to us showing His scars.

I hadn't known that full cruciformity looked fully like this. To give someone your broken heart means breaking pride, breaking lies, breaking fear. There's no communion unless someone breaks their ego. All along, had I only been scratching the surface of what it meant to be broken and given? How had I not lived like the brokenness itself is a gift?

Why not embrace the life work of embracing suffering, embracing brokenness? Why avoid the gift of more God, more vulnerability, more intimacy, more communion—the gifts that brokenheartedness offers? Why had I found that terrifying to incarnate? Suffering is a call for presence; it's a call for us to be present—not only to the brokenness in the world, but to the brokenness in our own soul, and to risk trusting others with our wounds. I think that is what's terrified me—trusting others with my wounds.

I text back to Mei:

I've lived given into people's brokenness. But I'm not sure I've known what it means to live given—actually giving my own brokenness? I don't think I've ever seen it as clearly as right now—being broken and given— means trusting enough to be vulnerable—and give your own brokenness.

Mei's words are steady, sure.

You have to be given. You.

I sit there holding her words in the open palm of my hand.

The way to live with your one broken heart—is to give it away. *What you need to give is your own brokenness.* A car out front turns a corner. How do you trust enough? How do you feel safe enough to trust enough? Mei's words unfold on the screen in my hand:

Hey . . . when you give your brokenness? You don't have to bang or break down any door to get in. You have a key. Always here. All access. All in. Always safe.

She was giving me a key? After all I'd done to show her I wasn't good at this?

The cross lit up on top of the steeple down the street keeps me company. Could I keep company with this way of His? To be with Him as He brings communion to my wounds? The stars are so bright up there tonight.

Maybe us with broken hearts simply need that—key people who break us open to see how Christ never stops holding our wounds, to break us free from all the crushing expectations, key people who simply say, "Come, it's safe to be real here, safe to let the brokenness come." Who doesn't need key people who free us from the old courtrooms where judgment and the scales of perfection have felt like millstones around our breaking necks? There isn't one of us who doesn't need key people who believe that the broken are the most beloved, that the busted are the brave, that the limping can lead—and that everything that looks like it's breaking apart might actually be falling together.

And isn't this what I've been longing to be—broken and broken free to be a key person? One of the soul emancipators who unleash others into who they are already in Him, no judging skeletons in closets or the size of a waist or the performance of anyone's kids or anything that might threaten to break us. Maybe—we become a key person when we hand a key to break someone free . . . *by giving each other our broken hearts.*

It's always the vulnerable heart that breaks broken hearts free.

Am I brave enough . . . to live not afraid of broken things?

Mei was handing me a key.

Mei? You have a key too. I'm handing you a key. And a commitment. My commitment to be a brokenhearted key person.

Kai rolls over in bed, thin arm with hospital wristband across the pillow. Brave and busted. *Let the brokenness come.* Stop holding on to a standard of perfection instead of being held by the arms of grace. Let your brokenness heal you in the strangest way. *Let it come, let it come.* How long had I felt perfectionism like a soundless strangle? Perfectionism is slow death by self. Perfectionism will kill your sense of safety, your self, your soul. Perfectionism isn't a fruit of the Spirit—joy is. Patience is. Peace is.

If I have loved others breathing in grace, why would I deny myself the same oxygen? And if I have needed to breathe in grace for me, how can I deny anyone needing the same oxygen?

Let all our brokenness be met by grace for all of us. We might breathe it in—and the pain might wane.

I reach out and barely touch my reflection in the window-pane. Judging is a blindfold. Judging others blinds us to our own grime—and to the grace that others are as needy of as we are.

Grace makes you safe. I type it out:

A few key people could change the world . . . If we
all had a few. And if we all were a key person, if we
were safe enough to receive broken hearts, if we were
brave enough to lay our broken heart right down on
the table—there'd be this breaking free. Given . . . if we
could just live given.

All the thousand roads and broken ways were leading here: Live *given*.

It's like the cross on my wrist pulses through my skin with that one word, like everything moves and falls down around and breathes and orbits and spins and unfurls and breaks free with that one word beating like a cry at the brave center of everything: *Given. Given.* Here is my brokenness. Given. Here is my battered life, here is my bruised control, here are my fractured dreams, here is my open hand, here is all that I have, here is my fragile, surrendered heart, here I am, a living sacrifice. Broken. Given.

Living given is more than giving your skills and your resources and your time and your hands and feet. Living given means breaking down all the thickened walls and barriers around your heart with this hammer of humility and trusting the expansiveness of the broken-wide-open spaces of grace and communion. *Can I do this?*

Unguarded, arms stretched out in widest surrender. Cruci-form. Given. This is freedom. *So why do I feel just a little bit like I can't breathe?*

Mei's words unfold in my hand.

When you are safe, when you have a few key people, choosing to live given is the best thing you could ever do.

Why does the head know what makes the heart choke a little bit?

I look back out the window. It's wide open out here, broken with no walls. And it's terrifying. And it's more beautiful than I could have ever known.

The whole sky to the southwest opens like an ombré canvas to the heavens above glowing town lights blinking off in the falling snow.

My heart tries to find words, form for the feelings.

Living given means that people will see the broken shards, the vulnerable edges of your given heart . . . and that means nothing less than radical humility and expansive trust.

When Mei's words reach me, they walk right in through fractures.

Yeah. It does mean all that. Living given is giving the brokenhearted your brokenness. And not being afraid of theirs.

A car turns into the hospital parking lot below, headlights rending the dark and all the shaking down snow.

Ann? I'm not scared of your broken, vulnerable edges. I'm not scared of being cut.

The room goes unstable, and tectonic plates shift inside me. It's like my whole world's a bucket flipped, upended. In one sentence, I see all this broken I've been trying to keep hidden fall away.

I look back down, read the line again. Run my fingers across it like it's braille and I'm just now able to see.

"I'm not scared of being cut."

My whole life I think I've been exactly that: afraid of being cut.

Afraid of being cut—and afraid of letting my sharp edges cut others . . . so they'd reject me, which would cut even deeper.

I lean back in the unsteady vinyl hospital chair. Kai's breathing heavy in sleep. Somewhere an alarm goes off, signaling an empty IV bag. That day I stood as a four-year-old kid and watched my sister's skull crack and break and bleed under the wheels of a delivery truck in our farmyard—I think I learned it first then. In a breaking world, you can find yourself shrinking back from the razor edge of broken things. Smashing glass on concrete at sixteen and kneeling down into shards to slice my begging skin—maybe it was about trying to cut through the brokenness that was breaking me, trying to bleed out the brokenness. Maybe when pain comes looking for you and you feel out of control, maybe you try to control the pain by going looking for it. Fear can drive you straight into things that will break you more. Was life about a movement exchanging bad brokenness . . . with knowing you've been chosen for good brokenness?

All that strangling anxiety, the agoraphobia that choked me into my twenties, I was driven by fear into believing I had to be perfect. *Perfectionism had killed my sense of safety, my sanctuary, my soul.*

The anger that simmered for years over the kid paraphernalia that littered the house and to-do lists that imploded—wasn't it always my fear of being broken? When the fear of not being enough haunts your days, isn't it, under everything, a fear of brokenness? This falling prey to performance and perfectionism and negativism was really a fear of falling into brokenness.

I think maybe—at the root of all control-wrestling and stress lies a fear of brokenness. Everything never made, never dreamed, never risked, never tried was because of a fear of brokenness. If there was too high a chance that the dream, the hope, the plan, might break, maybe it was just a failure I couldn't risk. And what made my life tight, what made my life anxious, what had made my life closed off and broken in a thousand ways, was merely that: fear of brokenness.

Everything in life that has ever been broken . . . has been because of fear of brokenness.

I want to lay my head down on something, let the emotion come.

Fear of brokenness has pushed away everything I have ever wanted, everything I have loved. It's been my very fear of brokenness that has caused unspoken brokenness. It was that: fear of brokenness has kept me from so much living; it has kept me from so much loving.

I sit, waiting. What happens when you realize that most of your life has been driven by fear of brokenness? The snow's falling heavier now. A nurse makes her rounds down the hall, cart rattling. *What is fear of brokenness but fear of suffering?*

If I have feared brokenness, suffering, all my life . . . does that mean I have sought my own comfort more than I have sought Christ? To fear suffering can be a fear of communion. A fear of Jesus and His ways of love. Whatever's breaking up across the breadth of me hurts like relief. I could heal. Kai rolls over in the heaviness of dreams, drapes his hand from the side of the bed. I reach over, take his hand, trace the lines in his palm. Wasn't it like an offering everywhere: brokenness offers closeness.

> For as we share abundantly in Christ's sufferings, so through Christ we share abundantly in comfort too.[2]

> We are . . . fellow heirs with Christ, provided we suffer with him in order that we may also be glorified with him.[3]

> My goal is to know Him, and the power of His resurrection and the fellowship of His sufferings, being conformed to His death.[4]

> Be very glad—for these trials make you partners with Christ in his suffering, so that you will have the wonderful joy of seeing his glory when it is revealed to all the world.[5]

Without an intimate fellowship with Christ's sufferings—how can there be intimate love with Christ? Refusing to be identified with the sufferings of Christ refuses any identity in Christ. I can feel Kai's pulse there under mine. No fear of the brokenness. No fear of the brokenness. It's beating right there under that cross that's brand-marked into me, and I'm learning to listen to it more than anything else. *Given. Given. Union with Christ in sufferings, communion with Christ in all things.*

Never be afraid of broken things—because Christ is redeeming everything.

Snowflakes melt down the window in this steady cadence. The abiding light of the town clock tower reflects like assurance in the long hospital window stretched to the side of Kai's bed. A truck waits at the end of the street, taillights blinking.

Oswald Chambers wrote, "God's way is always the way of suffering—the way of the 'long long trail.'"[6] God's way is always the broken way. For all my prayers and efforts to be broken and given for the suffering of the world, there'd been parts of me still terrified of suffering, avoiding it, still resisting being surrendered and broken and given. But now that is all I want. I want to be part of the fellowship of the broken. The fellowship of the broken believe that suffering is a gift He entrusts to us and He can be trusted to make this suffering into a gift. The fellowship of the broken take up the fearless broken way, are not afraid of brokenness, and don't need to try to fix anyone's brokenness, or try to hide it or judge it or mask it or exile it. This gift of Mei's, it's like my ceiling has become an open sky: I can break open my hand and my need to control because I'm no longer afraid of broken things. *Never be afraid of broken things—because Christ can redeem anything.* When I'm no longer afraid of brokenness, I don't have to control or possess anything—dreams or plans or people or their perceptions. I can live surrendered. Cruciform. Given. This feels like freedom.

Not being afraid of the brokenness—*this sets you free in a thousand ways.*

Free! FREE! Free to simply sit with brokenness and feel a

brokenhearted Healer come closer even now, especially now, to cup the broken hearts laid out on the table.

I run my fingers through Malakai's hair. Slowly, thoughtfully. Maybe not being afraid of the brokenness ultimately means—not even fearing the fear of brokenness. There it is, what could be: do not even fear being afraid of the brokenness; no longer let fear control any part of you, paralyze you, or drive you.

The thought comes like something falling softly from beyond the sky: there is no self-chastising or self-castigating or self-berating for even being afraid of brokenness. Maybe I had finally come to the place where I could see myself, my brokenness, my fear of brokenness, with the same tender compassion with which Jesus sees all of me. Maybe the broken way leads to being as compassionate with yourself as Jesus is with your soul, granting yourself the grace He gives, grace to get it wrong and grace to change again, grace to be broken and broken again, and the grace to grow and grow on, like the broken way of seeds.

Maybe not being afraid of even the fear of brokenness allows you to feel the fear and know it's okay because you're never alone in your fear. You are never alone, never abandoned, never not safe. He gives us what we need most to fight the fear: *communion*. Comfort your fears with more of Him, with touching His own broken heart, by letting Him gently press your wounds into His. With-ness breaks brokenness. He comes again, always again, Jesus whispering over everything else, "Do not be afraid—I am with you." Koinonia *is always, always the miracle*.

When you know you're never alone in the fear, you lose the fear of the fear. Not being afraid of even being afraid—may be the bravest way of all.

All there ever is to see is Jesus. All there ever is to hear is "Beloved."

This feels like a resurrection, like stars breaking dark, like holy redemption, a rising of life breaking out of its seed sheath.

Kai turns. The hospital bed jangles. Mei's words come quietly.

> Living given? Means those rough, sharp vulnerable
> edges are out there exposed to the heart that's
> holding them. Which means? We will get cut.

I reach out to pick up her words, cross at the wrist slipping out my sleeve.

> Ironically? You cut people the deepest when you try to
> keep your vulnerability the most hidden.

The snow squalls have quieted. The stars seem clear, close.

> But hear me: I am Not. Afraid. To. Be. Cut.

I sit at the window with her words, Kai breathing slow in sleep.

But before I can tell her what her words have meant to me, what's happened here—

> And I don't know if you know it or not? But you aren't
> either.

Epilogue

O Spirit, beautiful and dread!
My heart is fit to break
With love of all Thy tenderness
For us poor sinners' sake.

FREDERICK FABER

It took more than a coon's age, but the results came back today that there's finally enough iron in my blood. Like something had, finally, bled down into the veins, got into the chambers, and made me live.

Malakai has needled himself almost a thousand times now, injecting insulin into his body to stay alive. This is how we keep learning to live: stay weak and dependent to stay strong.

I'd sat today in the waiting room beside a woman who told me she had just buried her husband. Lou Gehrig's disease and a protracted death wrestle. I watched her grip the armrests until her knuckles turned white and I tried to hear all the things she didn't find words for. Her open face turned to me. "I cared for him right till the end . . ." Her eyes drifted off like she'd seen behind the veil.

"This is all I know now about living: Every moment is a gift with each other—and every moment we get to be a gift to each other. *This is all there is.*"

I nodded, holding her gaze, gave forward the gift of presence—because I knew a broken story kind of like that, of one broken woman reaching out to touch the intimate communion of the cross, and finding in it the form of a life—cruciform. Love comes down, a gift, and grateful *eucharisteo* rises back to Him. And then *koinonia* love, broken and given as the gift, reaches out to an aching world—even, especially, with bits of our broken self. *Cruciform.*

Eucharisteo had led me to *koinonia*—was it so surprising? When you feel a radical gratitude for what you have, you end up wanting to go to radical lengths to share it. When you are radically grateful for being blessed, you want to be radically generous to the oppressed. Because you know that is the way to radical abundance—there's always more for more to share the grace.

We are where we are to risk everything for those outside the gate, because we are *one* with the broken—all gates that divide us are mirage. Comfort and affluence can make you blind. Blind to the hungry Christ, the thirsty, suffering, broken Christ. Isn't this why it's hard for the comfortable to experience authentic abundance—because they're blinded to Christ?

I'd reached out my hand to hold the grieving widow's. *Willing to be broken into. Broken and given. This is all there is.* Those who claim Christ aren't only saved by a crucified Savior; their lives are *shaped* by Him.

The cross isn't some cheap symbol of faith; it's the exact shape we embody as the life of Christ. When we won't see the suffering—who are *all* of us—we never form our lives like our Savior's.

A Christ-shaped life is not a comfortably shaped life, but a cross-shaped life.

I'd come home from the doctor's office, laid my bag there on the dining room buffet by my busted Lord's Supper sculpture. He's right there, kneeling, hands cut off, ever beckoning. Had my own hands had to be broken free of performance, of idols, of convenience, of perfectionism, to stop being afraid to be cut or wounded, to stop fearing the suffering of broken things? Had I had to feel the depths of my own insufficient and brokenness to allow a deeper abundance to come?

The sun dips toward the golden hour and I wander out toward the wheat because I need . . . I need to stretch out my arms and feel the whole expanse of the flung sky, the ocean of rolling wheat breaking free, feel how fear is executed with one line: *there is enough.* Run through the gilded stalks and feel how all fear shrivels when you serenade your heart with one refrain: *there is abundance.* There is always more because God is always enough, and He makes all brokenness into abundance and never be afraid of broken things because Christ is redeeming everything. Run and feel the bowed heads open the way: "The LORD is indeed going before you—he will be with you; he will not fail you or abandon you. Do not be afraid."[1] Run, and the sky and a thousand cups of light break overhead: You can abandon all your cares because Christ will never, ever abandon you. You can abandon your fears and abide in the safe expanse of Your Father.

The fading dome of blue sky over the gold stretches over me, over everything, His shielding roof, *stego*, protected in His unending love, and the evening breeze exhales the secret to relief: the soul is broken free when we're freed of self and abandoned to the will of God.

Hope's coming across the fields to me, her hair falling long across her shoulders, the color of wheat. The woods fall away behind us. When she reaches me, she reaches for my hand, smiles, and we hold on to each other and run, laughing, lifted into the rustle of all this willing surrender making abundance. Can I memorize her here with me, our with-ness breaking brokenness? Oh, this long way we'd come through brokenness is the essence of humanness, and fragility is the beating heart of humanity, and accepting that without shame is the beginning of freedom. Brokenness doesn't need shame or guilt—brokenness needs to be shared and given. Broken and given and shared with Jesus, and with a world that needs to embrace weakness to embrace abundance. She doesn't let go of my hand.

This deeper communion with God I'd been after, the question of how to live with brokenness, it's remade me, reformed me, reshaped me—again. I am found to the extent I keep *koinonia* with the broken because He loves best those who need Him most. It's whispering through wheat and ringing loud in my soul. *What do you do with your brokenness?* Give your one broken heart away. *What's the answer to suffering in this world?* Destroy it with co-suffering, with compassion, with givenness. Bad brokenness is always broken by good brokenness. Your life turns around when you refuse to turn away from brokenness.

Hope keeps turning, finding my eyes, smiling, and I hold her hand tighter, her a blazing Esther, giving herself and risking loving me, even me. Sun's broken into the wheat, indwells all the wheat, and we're running straight into all the light, the heads of wheat brushing the scars on my wrist, the cross on my wrist, her hand in mine, a blur of scars, thousands upon thousands of bowed heads ready to yield breathing it: *Givenness. Givenness.* This is communion. This is freedom. Union with Him, with His Beloved. And there is no stopping the breaking free. I could trust enough to give, give Him forward, give even my own brokenness, and not be afraid it would break anyone—because brokenness makes communion. Brokenness makes abundance. The aloneness and disconnect and abandonment felt from the beginning, it is counteracted in communion, a way of giving and sharing that requires the intimacy of brokenness. It's happening all around us and I can almost see it: once you dare to take the broken way, stay with the broken, daily give forward even your brokenness, your broken heart is enlightened, it becomes light. Your heart learns a new way of being—a paradoxical abundant broken way. It can only be learned in *koinonia*, with Christ and with His body. Communion is our course to abundance. Communion is the way Jesus ultimately came to show us, because ultimately, the givenness of communion is the essence of really living. *Koinonia* is always, always the miracle and there is no other way to enter abundance.

Hope and I are about out of breath, but filled, wheat humming in the rush of our running, hearts pounding alive in our ears. I was born in the middle of a wheat harvest and all this gold will be harvested tomorrow and its kernels will run through our open hands. There isn't one stalk in this field that's afraid to be cut.

It's the broken hearts that find the haunting loveliness of a new beat—it's the broken hearts that live a song that echoes God's.

> Beat, beloved heart, beat on in the world.
> You will be broken and you will be loved.
> You don't ever have to be afraid.

> The way keeps opening up before us.
> And we'll let it come.

Acknowledgments

To these, who gave me the miracle of *koinonia*, communion I didn't deserve, I humbly offer up the two most profound, potent words I know: *Thank you.*

To Bill Jensen for his protecting kindness; Holly Good for always being willing, available, and like Jesus; Tom Dean, Robin Barnett, John Raymond, Dirk Buursma, Ted Barnett, and Jennifer Tucker for not only being a dream team, but a team who pours out everything for God's dream for the world.

To Mick and Sheri Silva, who believe in the broken and bind up the wounded and never give up on those who've fallen down—it wouldn't have been possible without you.

To Sandy Vander Zicht, a tireless prayer warrior, relentless champion, gold-medal editor, and faithful friend—you're everything an author ever hopes to experience. There aren't enough words to express my gratitude.

To every single sojourner and reader who's thrown in and traveled with our brave and busted online community, who's shared a bit of their unspoken broken with me, who's risen up as a GenEsther, who's poured their bucket right out into abundance, who's had the courage of stars and lived with their one broken heart by giving it away, who's shared our community and welcomed one more into the beauty of the broken way—you are forever my people. These pages are for you and because of you and let's never stop doing *koinonia* together until Kingdom Come.

To Lisa-Jo Baker, Rebekah Lyons, Scott Sauls, Liz Curtis Higgs, Jessica Turner, and Meredith Toering, who are the uncommon heroes and brought cup after cup of His light—you incarnate Jesus to me and I'll never be done thanking Him for you. Mei, you helped me find broken pieces of me and gave me more of Him.

To Mark Buchanan, Jon and Pam Bloom, Marvin Olasky, Gene Edward Veith, Tony Reinke, Sheila Walsh, Lysa TerKeurst, Philip Yancey, Bill and Gloria Gaither, Randy and Nancy Alcorn, Louie and Shelley Giglio, David and Heather Platt, Max Lucado, Timothy Keller, Sally Lloyd-Jones, Beth Moore, Christine Caine, Kay Warren, Patsy Clairmont, Lisa Harper, Amena Brown Owen, Jason Gray, Scot McKnight, Deidra Riggs, Melanie Shankle, Sophie Hudson, and Mary Anne Morgan—each of you mended deeply broken places with words that were a healing balm, with friendship that's drenched with the scent of God, with grace that's shaped like Christ's. You will never know how He used each of you and how indebted I will go to the grave.

To Shaun Groves, Steve and Patricia Jones, and Keely Scott—you welcomed us into the Compassion family and gave us a way to be broken and given . . . in Jesus' name. You've opened the door into a giving joy that blew up our hearts. Kristen and Terrell Welch and Mike Rusch and the Mercy House Global family—you lead the broken way, and serving with you, for such a time as this, multiplies time.

For Emilie Wierda and Kathie Lee Gifford, for extending such a generous, faithful hand of friendship that has been a guidepost on the way. Your constant support's been the most humbling grace.

Acknowledgments

For Lauren and Matt Chandler, Gabe and Rebekah Lyons, Jen and Brandon Hatmaker, Angie and Todd Smith, Lindsey Nobles, Esther Havens, Jennie and Zac Allen, who know you are here for such a time as this, who do whatever it takes to tear down gates, who lead GenEsthers to risk everything, because if we don't, we perish—serving with you is a kind of communion with Christ.

For Sherri and Ron Martin, Marlene and Randy Fitch, Gary and Diane Goodkey, Pete and Ang Koobs, Elizabeth Foss and Ginny Foreman, who have loved us when it was inconvenient, showed up when it was unexpected, and been the kind of friends who go the whole long way.

For DaySpring's (in)courage family of writers and friends— each one of you are home to me and ushered me into the miracle of *koinonia*.

For David, Noa and Mya, Lia and Ana, Ema and Eli—that we get to be family and take The Way together. I love you.

For Molly, the sister I couldn't have lived without; for John, the brother who has prayed and loved relentlessly; for my dad, who has kept loving through busted places; and for my mama, who is a Real Velveteen Mama and the most soul-beautiful mama I could have ever hoped for.

For Caleb, Joshua, Hope, Levi, Malakai, Shalom, and Shiloh, our seven sent from heaven—your love has loosened me into Real and loving you all has been the greatest reward of all.

For Darryl, a cruciform man who has made himself into *stego*, a roof for me to feel safe under—your love has healed wounds.

For God the Father, God the Son, and God the Holy Spirit . . . who beckons the abandoned into union and *koinonia*, woos us with intimate grace, and binds our wounds with His broken and given heart so we are bound forever and broken free.

Bible Translations Cited

Notes

CHAPTER 1: WHAT TO DO WITH YOUR ONE BROKEN HEART

1. Victor Hugo, *Les Misérables* (New York: Carleton, 1863), 127.
2. Matthew 27:46.
3. Matthew 9:12.
4. John 9:3 MSG.
5. John 9:3 NLT.
6. Mother Teresa, *Come Be My Light: The Private Writings of the Saint of Calcutta*, ed. Brian Kolodiejchuk (New York: Doubleday, 2007), 149, 185, 212.
7. Isaiah 61:1.
8. Charles H. Spurgeon, "Christ's Hospital: A Sermon on Psalm 147:3," *Metropolitan Tabernacle Pulpit*, www .spurgeon.org/sermons/2260.php (accessed June 3, 2016).

CHAPTER 2: RE-MEMBERING YOUR BROKEN PIECES

1. Luke 22:19.
2. Augustine, *Confessions*, trans. R. S. Pine-Coffin (New York: Penguin, 1961), 228 (X, 21).
3. This paragraph and the preceding six paragraphs are based on a section in my *One Thousand Gifts* (Grand Rapids: Zondervan, 2010), 31–33.
4. Luke 22:19.

5. Matthew 15:36.
6. Quoted in Vanessa Thorpe, "Magic Realism . . . and Fakery," *Guardian online*, January 21, 2001, www.theguardian.com/world/2001/jan/21/books.booksnews (accessed June 3, 2016).

CHAPTER 3: WHEN YOU WANT TO EXCHANGE YOUR BROKENNESS

1. John 12:24 ESV.
2. John 12:25 MSG.
3. See Timothy Keller, "The Gospel and Sex," www.christ2 rculture.com/resources/Ministry-Blog/The-Gospel-and-Sex -by-Tim-Keller.pdf (accessed June 3, 2016).
4. Martin Luther, "Treatise on Christian Liberty (1520)," http://history.hanover.edu/courses/excerpts/165luther.html (accessed June 3, 2016).
5. Ibid.
6. Martin Luther, quoted in Alister E. McGrath, *Christian Spirituality: An Introduction* (New York: Oxford, 1999), 158–59.
7. Luther, "Treatise on Christian Liberty."
8. A. M. Stibbs, *Sacrament, Sacrifice, and Eucharist* (London: Tyndale Press, 1961), 75.
9. D. Martyn Lloyd-Jones, *Spiritual Depression: Its Causes and Cure* (Grand Rapids: Eerdmans, 1965), 74–75.
10. Ephesians 2:14, my paraphrase.
11. 2 Peter 1:4 NASB.
12. John 14:23.
13. Psalm 63:1.

CHAPTER 4: HOW TO BREAK TIME IN TWO

1. A. W. Tozer, *God's Pursuit of Man* (1950; repr., Chicago: Moody, 2015), 20.

2. C. S. Lewis, *The Screwtape Letters* (1976; repr., Grand Rapids: Revell, 1994), 127.
3. John 12:24 ESV.
4. John 17:1, paraphrase.
5. 1 Corinthians 13:8 MSG.

CHAPTER 5: BECOMING THE GIFT THE WORLD NEEDS—AND YOU NEED

1. John 3:16, my paraphrase, emphasis mine.
2. Charles Haddon Spurgeon, *John Ploughman's Talk: Or, Advice for Plain People* (1868; repr., Eugene, OR: Wipf & Stock, 2006), 139.
3. Isaiah 58:7–9 MSG.
4. Saint Augustine of Hippo, "Exposition II, Sermon I on Psalm 30," in *Expositions on the Book of Psalms*, vol. 1 (Oxford: Parker, 1847), 249.
5. Luke 22:19; 1 Corinthians 10:16, my paraphrase.
6. A. W. Tozer, *The Pursuit of God* (1948; repr., Abbotsford, WI: Aneko, 2015), 11, 19.
7. Simone Weil, *Waiting for God* (1951; repr., New York: HarperCollins, 2001), 104.
8. See S. Lyubomirsky, K. M. Sheldon, and D. Schkade, "Pursuing Happiness: The Architecture of Sustainable Change," *Review of General Psychology* 9: 111–31; Danica Collins, "The Act of Kindness and Its Positive Health Benefits," June 8, 2011, http://undergroundhealth reporter.com/act-of-kindness (accessed June 3, 2016).
9. C. H. Spurgeon, *Morning by Morning: Or Daily Readings for the Family or the Closet* (New York: Sheldon, 1866), October 26, 300.
10. Proverbs 11:25 HCSB.

11. Luke 6:38 MSG.

12. C. S. Lewis, *Mere Christianity* (1952; repr., New York: HarperCollins, 2001), 199.

13. Martin Luther, "The Freedom of a Christian (1520)," www.spucc.org/sites/default/files/Luther%20Freedom.pdf (accessed June 3, 2016).

14. Isaiah 58:10.

15. Lewis, *Mere Christianity*, 177, 199.

16. Dietrich Bonhoeffer, *The Cost of Discipleship* (1949; repr., New York: Macmillan, 1963), 99.

17. Lewis, *Mere Christianity*, 196.

18. Ibid., 196–97.

19. Ibid., 197.

20. Ibid., 197–98.

CHAPTER 6: WHAT'S EVEN BETTER THAN A BUCKET LIST

1. 1 Corinthians 1:9, my paraphrase.

2. Isaiah 42:3.

3. Isaiah 61:1.

4. Richard Sibbes, *The Bruised Reed and Smoking Flax* (Philadelphia: Presbyterian Board of Publication, 1620), 100.

5. Romans 8:39.

6. Michael Woody, "The Bucket List," *American Way*, August 15, 2012, www.ink-live.com/emagazines/american -way/2065/august-2012-2/files/assets/common/downloads/ AW20120815.pdf (accessed June 3, 2016).

7. Viktor E. Frankl, *Man's Search for Meaning* (New York: Simon and Schuster, 1985), 133.

8. Philippians 2:5–8 AMP.

9. Matthew 25:34–36, 44–45 MSG.

10. Galatians 2:19; 5:24; 6:14.
11. 2 Corinthians 4:7–15.

CHAPTER 7: LOVE IS A ROOF FOR ALL OUR BROKENNESS

1. Romans 5:8.
2. 1 Corinthians 13:7 ESV.
3. 1 John 3:16.

CHAPTER 8: WHY LOVE IS WORTH BREAKING YOUR HEART

1. Ayn Rand, *The Fountainhead* (Indianapolis: Bobbs-Merrill, 1943), 677.
2. Matthew 16:25.

CHAPTER 9: THE MIRACLE IN YOUR POCKET THAT BREAKS STRESS

1. See Mary Brophy Marcus, "Doing Small Acts of Kindness May Lower Your Stress," *CBS News.com*, December 15, 2015, www.cbsnews.com/news/doing-small-acts-of-kind ness-may-lower-your-own-stress (accessed June 3, 2016).
2. Simone Weil, from an April 13, 1942, letter to poet Joë Bousquet, published in their collected correspondence (*Correspondance* [Lausanne: Editions l'Age d'Homme, 1982], 18).
3. Saint Ignatius, in a Letter to Ascanio Colonna (Rome, April 25, 1543), quoted in "Abandoning Ourselves to His Hands," Bishop Felipe J. Estévez, *St. Augustine Catholic* (September/October 2014), 7, http://faithdigital.org/ staugustine/SA0914/03197846597C1F18B6D8F09EB9 D106CC/SA1014.pdf (accessed June 3, 2016).

4. Marcus, "Doing Small Acts of Kindness May Lower Your Stress."
5. Ibid.
6. C. S. Lewis, *The Problem of Pain* (New York: Macmillan, 1962), 152.

CHAPTER 10: HOW TO PASSIONATELY LOVE WHEN YOUR HEART'S BREAKING

1. John 16:20 HCSB.

CHAPTER 11: BREAKING INTO BEING REAL

1. Genesis 3:1.
2. Romans 8:35, 37–39.
3. Quoted in Charles J. Healy, *Praying with the Jesuits: Finding God in All Things* (Mahwah, NJ: Paulist, 2011), 45.
4. Genesis 37–50.
5. Margery Williams, *The Velveteen Rabbit* (1922; repr., New York: Holt, 1983), 4–5.
6. Psalm 51:17 MSG, HCSB.
7. Mark 8:34–37 MSG, emphasis mine.

CHAPTER 12: BREAKING YOUR BROKENNESS

1. Martin Luther, quoted in *Text-Book of the History of Doctrines*, vol. 1, Reinhold Seeberg (Eugene, OR: Wipf & Stock, 1997), 236.
2. Mark 1:15.
3. Thomas Howard and J. I. Packer, *Christianity: The True Humanism* (Vancouver, BC: Regent College Publishing, 1985), 153.
4. Galatians 6:9 MSG.

CHAPTER 13: THE INCONVENIENT TRUTH NO ONE TELLS YOU

1. Kara Tippetts, "Abiding," *Mundane Faithfulness* blog post, February 17, 2015, www.mundanefaithfulness.com/home/2015/2/17/abiding (accessed July 15, 2016).

2. "The Great Litany," *The Online Book of Common Prayer*, www.bcponline.org/GreatLitany/Litany2.html (accessed July 15, 2016).

3. Peter Kreeft, *Making Sense Out of Suffering* (Ann Arbor, MI: Servant, 1986), 137.

4. Eugene Peterson, "Introduction to the Books of Moses," in *The Message: The Bible in Contemporary Language* (Colorado Springs: NavPress, 2002), 17.

5. Nicholas Wolterstorff, *Lament for a Son* (Grand Rapids: Eerdmans, 1987), 84.

6. Romans 12:13 ESV.

7. Luke 22:19.

8. Hebrews 10:33, emphasis mine.

9. Psalm 90:12, my paraphrase.

10. Charles Haddon Spurgeon, *Spurgeon's Sermons on Great Prayers of the Bible* (Grand Rapids: Kregel, 1995), 31.

11. Elisabeth Elliot, quoted in Gateway to Joy, "The Furnace of Affliction," *Back to the Bible*, http://web.archive.org/web/20140818143351/http://www.backtothebible.org:80/index.php/Gateway-to-Joy/Defining-Suffering.html (accessed June 3, 2016).

12. Martin Luther, "Preface to Romans (1552)," 2, www.messiahskingdom.com/resources/The-Gospel/luther-romans.pdf (accessed June 3, 2016).

CHAPTER 14: BREAKING THE LIES IN YOUR HEAD

1. John 9:3, my paraphrase.
2. Søren Kierkegaard, *The Sickness Unto Death* (Princeton, NJ: Princeton University Press, 1941), 130, 132.
3. Timothy Keller, *The Reason for God: Belief in an Age of Skepticism* (New York: Dutton, 2008), 162.
4. Hebrews 13:6 MSG.
5. Isaiah 44:20.
6. Martin Luther, "Treatise on Christian Liberty (1520)," http://history.hanover.edu/courses/excerpts/165luther.html (accessed June 3, 2016).
7. Karl Barth, *Church Dogmatics*, vol. 4, part 3.2, "The Doctrine of Reconciliation" (Edinburgh: T&T Clark, 1988), 549.
8. Isaiah 44:20.

CHAPTER 15: HOW TO BE AN ESTHER AND BREAK A THOUSAND GATES

1. Elisabeth Elliot, *These Strange Ashes* (1998; repr., Grand Rapids: Revell, 2004), 145.
2. Esther 4:13–14 NLT.
3. Mark 8:36, my paraphrase.
4. Timothy Keller, *Generous Justice: How God's Grace Makes Us Just* (New York: Dutton, 2012), 177.
5. Ibid., 177, 180.
6. Isaiah 53:3 ESV.
7. Matthew 10:42; 25:40, my paraphrase.
8. Matthew 25:43, my paraphrase.
9. Henri Nouwen, *Gracias: A Latin American Journal* (New York: Harper & Row, 1983), 20.
10. Luke 14:12–14 HCSB.

11. J. H. van den Berg, *A Different Existence* (Pittsburgh: Duquesne University Press, 1972), 105.
12. Peter Leithart, *Traces of the Trinity: Signs of God in Creation and Human Experience* (Grand Rapids: Brazos, 2015), 137.

CHAPTER 16: WHEN IT COMES TO WOOING GOD AND HEALING WOUNDS

1. C. S. Lewis, *The Screwtape Letters* (1976; repr., Grand Rapids: Revell, 1994), 51.
2. John Piper, "Call Me Husband, Not Baal," www.desiring god.org/messages/call-me-husband-not-baal (accessed June 3, 2016).
3. Matthew 25:35–36, 40 MSG.
4. "Come, Ye Sinners, Poor and Wretched," lyrics by Joseph Hart (1759). Public domain.
5. C. S. Lewis, *Letters to Malcolm: Chiefly on Prayer* (New York: Harcourt, Brace & World, 1964), 91.

CHAPTER 17: HOW TO FIND THE HEROES IN A SUFFERING WORLD

1. 1 Kings 18:28.
2. Charles H. Spurgeon, "The Compassion of Jesus: A Sermon," *Metropolitan Tabernacle Pulpit*, www.spurgeon.org/ sermons/3438.php (accessed June 3, 2016).
3. P. J. O'Rourke, *All the Trouble in the World* (New York: Atlantic Monthly Press, 1994), 9, my paraphrase.
4. Matthew 9:36 KJV.
5. Psalm 90:13.
6. Isaiah 49:13 ESV.
7. See Exodus 34:6.

8. This "song" is based on Isaiah 49:15–16; Matthew 9:36; Luke 15:3–7; John 10:1–18; 2 Corinthians 1:3–4.
9. Isaiah 44:5.

CHAPTER 18: WHY YOU DON'T HAVE TO BE AFRAID TO BE BROKEN

1. Søren Kierkegaard, *Repetition*, in *The Essential Kierkegaard*, ed. Howard V. Hong and Edna H. Hong (Princeton, NJ: Princeton University Press, 1978), 112.
2. 2 Corinthians 1:5 ESV.
3. Romans 8:16–17 ESV.
4. Philippians 3:10 HCSB.
5. 1 Peter 4:13 NLT.
6. Oswald Chambers, *My Utmost for His Highest* (London: Marshall, Morgan and Scott, 1927), 310.

EPILOGUE

1. Deuteronomy 31:8 NET.

The Broken Way
Study Guide
with DVD

Ann Voskamp

In this six-session video Bible
study, New York Times best-
selling author Ann Voskamp takes you on a personal journey
along the broken way. The broken way beckons you into more
time, more meaning, more authentic relationships. There's a
way, especially when things aren't shaping up quite like you
imagined, that makes life take the shape of more—more abundance, more intimacy, more God.

Ann Voskamp asks the following questions not one of us can
afford to ignore:

- How do you live your one broken life?
- What does it mean to live cruciform and learn to receive?
- What do you do if you really want to know abundant
  wholeness—before it's too late?

There's a way of honest, transformative power.
Dare to take the broken way—to abundance.

One Thousand Gifts

A Dare to Live Fully Right Where You Are

Ann Voskamp

Like most readers, Ann Voskamp hungers to live her one life well. Forget the bucket lists about once-in-a-lifetime experiences.

"How," Ann wondered, "do we find joy in the midst of deadlines, debt, drama, and daily duties? What does a life of gratitude look like when your days are gritty, long, and sometimes dark? What is God providing here and now?

A beautifully practical guide to living a life of joy, *One Thousand Gifts* invites you to wake up to God's everyday blessings. As Voskamp discovered, in giving thanks for the life she already had, she found the life she'd always wanted.

Following Voskamp's grace-bathed reflections on her farming, parenting, and writing life, you will embark on the transformative spiritual discipline of chronicling gifts. You will discover a way of seeing that opens your eyes to gratitude, a way of living so you are not afraid to die, and a way of becoming present to God's presence that brings deep and lasting happiness.

Also available:

One Thousand Gifts available in both blue and brown duotone leather editions

One Thousand Gifts: A DVD Study: A Dare to Live Fully Right Where You Are

One Thousand Gifts Devotional: Reflections on Finding Everyday Grace

Selections from One Thousand Gifts: Finding Joy in What Really Matters